• Personal performance (p. 66)

• SuperMemo (p. 62) • Elbæk (p. 56)

• Music matrix (p. 52)

gnitive dissonance (p. 50)

• Hype cycle (p. 74)

• Network target (p. 80) • Unimaginable (p. 54)

• Energy (p. 60)

• Making of (p. 68)

• Personal potential trap (p. 72)

Flow (p. 46)

• Political compass (p. 64) • Superficial knowledge (p. 82)

Subtle signals (p. 78)

• Johari window (p. 48)

• Fashion (p. 58)

THINKING

• A.I. (p. 102) • Sinus/Bourdieu (p. 94)

• Maslow (p. 90)

Small world (p. 104)

• Double loop (p. 98)

• Outside the box (p. 92)

• Status (p. 120)

• Pareto (p. 106)

• Black box (p. 118)

'risoner's dilemma (p. 124)

• Long tail (p. 108)

• Swiss cheese (p. 86) • Black swan (p. 112)

• Monte Carlo (p. 110)

• Chasm (p. 114)

ERS

HOW TO UNDERSTAND
OTHERS BETTER

THE DECISION BOOK

FIFTY MODELS FOR STRATEGIC THINKING

Mikael Krogerus
Roman Tschäppeler

Translated by Jenny Piening

WITH ILLUSTRATIONS BY PHILIP EARNHART

W. W. Norton & Company
New York • London

CONTENTS

Instructions for use 5

HOW TO IMPROVE YOURSELF

The Eisenhower matrix: *How to work more efficiently* 10
The SWOT analysis: *How to find the right solution* 12
The BCG box: *How to evaluate costs and benefits* 14
The project portfolio matrix: *How to maintain an overview* 16
The John Whitmore model: *Am I pursuing the right goal?* 20
The rubber band model: *How to deal with a dilemma* 22
The feedback model: *Dealing with other people's compliments and criticisms* 24
The family tree model: *The contacts you should maintain* 26
The morphological box and SCAMPER: *Why you have to be structured to be creative* 28
The *Esquire* gift model: *How much to spend on gifts* 32
The consequences model: *Why it is important to make decisions promptly* 34
The conflict resolution model: *How to resolve a conflict elegantly* 36
The crossroads model: *So what next?* 40

HOW TO UNDERSTAND YOURSELF BETTER

The flow model: *What makes you happy?* 46
The Johari window: *What others know about you* 48
The cognitive dissonance model: *Why people smoke when they know it's unhealthy* 50
The music matrix: *What your taste in music says about you* 52
The unimaginable model: *What do you believe in that you cannot prove?* 54
The Uffe Elbæk model: *How to get to know yourself* 56

The fashion model: *How we dress* 58
The energy model: *Are you living in the here and now?* 60
The SuperMemo model: *How to remember everything you have ever learned* 62
The political compass: *What political parties stand for* 64
The personal performance model: *How to recognise whether you should change your job* 66
The making-of model: *To determine your future, first understand your past* 68
The personal potential trap: *Why it is better not to expect anything* 72
The hype cycle: *How to identify the next big thing* 74
The subtle signals model: *Why nuances matter* 78
The network target model: *What your friends say about you* 80
The superficial knowledge model: *Everything you don't need to know* 82

HOW TO UNDERSTAND OTHERS BETTER

The Swiss cheese model: *How mistakes happen* 86
The Maslow pyramids: *What you actually need, what you actually want* 90
Thinking outside the box: *How to come up with brilliant ideas* 92
The Sinus Milieu and Bourdieu models: *Where you belong* 94
The double-loop learning model: *How to learn from your mistakes* 98
The AI model: *What kind of discussion type are you?* 102
The small-world model: *How small the world really is* 104
The Pareto principle: *Why 80 per cent of the output is achieved with 20 per cent of the input* 106
The long-tail model: *How the internet is transforming the economy* 108

The Monte Carlo simulation: *Why we can only approximate a definitive outcome* 110
The black swan model: *Why your experiences don't make you any wiser* 112
The chasm – the diffusion model: *Why everybody has an iPod* 114
The black box model: *Why faith is replacing knowledge* 118
The status model: *How to recognise a winner* 120
The prisoner's dilemma: *When is it worth trusting someone?* 124

HOW TO IMPROVE OTHERS

The Drexler–Sibbet team performance model: *How to turn a group into a team* 130
The team model: *Is your team up to the job?* 134
The gap-in-the-market model: *How to recognise a bankable idea* 136
The Hersey–Blanchard model (situational leadership): *How to successfully manage your employees* 138
The role-playing model: *How to change your own point of view* 142
The result optimisation model: *Why the printer always breaks down just before a deadline* 146
The world's next top model 148

NOW IT'S YOUR TURN

Drawing lesson 1 156
Drawing lesson 2 158
My models 160

APPENDIX

Bibliography 167
Illustration credits 169
Final note 171
Thanks 172
The authors 173

INSTRUCTIONS FOR USE

WHY YOU SHOULD READ THIS BOOK

This book has been written for anyone who has to deal with people on a daily basis. Whether you are a teacher, a professor, a pilot or a top manager, you will be confronted by the same questions time and again: How do I make the right decision? How can I motivate myself or my team? How can I change things? How can I work more efficiently? And on a more personal level: What do my friends reveal about me? Do I live in the here and now? What do I want?

WHAT YOU WILL FIND IN THIS BOOK

The fifty best decision-making models – well-known and not so well-known – that will help you tackle these questions are described in words and diagrams. Don't expect straight answers; be prepared to be tested. Expect food for thought. You will acquire the kind of knowledge with which you can impress friends and colleagues: What is a black swan? What is a long tail? What is the Pareto principle? Why do we always forget everything? How should I behave in conflict situations?

HOW TO USE THIS BOOK

This is a workbook. You can copy out the models, fill them in, cross them out, and develop and improve them. Whether you need to prepare for a presentation or carry out an annual performance review, whether a difficult decision lies ahead of you or a prolonged dispute is now behind you, whether you want to reassess your business idea or get to know yourself better – this book will guide you.

WHAT IS A DECISION-MAKING MODEL?

The models in this book fulfil the following criteria:

- They **simplify**: they do not embrace every aspect of reality, but only include those aspects that seem relevant.
- They are **pragmatic**: they focus on what is useful.
- They **sum up**: they are executive summaries of complex interrelations.
- They are **visual**: through images and diagrams, they convey concepts that are difficult to explain in words.
- They **organise**: they provide structure and create a filing system.
- They are **methods**: they do not provide answers, they ask questions; answers emerge once you have used the models, i.e. filled them out and worked with them.

In the appendix you will find the sources of the models, as well as references to books and websites. Models for which no source is given there have been developed by the authors.

WHY DO WE NEED DECISION-MAKING MODELS?

When we encounter chaos, we seek ways to structure it, to see through it, or at least to gain an overview of it. Models help us to reduce the complexity of a situation by enabling us to suppress most of it and concentrate on what is important. Critics like to point out that models do not reflect reality. That is true, but it is wrong to claim that they compel us to think in a prescribed way. Models do not define what or how we should think; they are the result of an active thought process.

You can read this book in the American or the European way. Americans tend towards a trial-and-error approach: they do something, fail, learn from this, acquire theories and try again. If this approach suits you, start at the beginning with 'How to improve yourself'. Europeans tend to begin by acquiring theories, then doing something. If they then fail, they analyse, improve and repeat the attempt. If this approach is more your style, begin with 'How to understand yourself better' (p.45).

Each model is only as good as the person who uses it.

HOW TO IMPROVE YOURSELF

THE EISENHOWER MATRIX

HOW TO WORK MORE EFFICIENTLY

The US President Dwight D. Eisenhower supposedly once said: 'The most urgent decisions are rarely the most important ones'. Eisenhower was considered a master of time management, i.e. he had the ability to do everything as and when it needed to be done. With the Eisenhower method, you will learn to distinguish between what is important and what is urgent.

Whatever the job that lands on your desk, begin by breaking it down according to the Eisenhower method (see model), and then decide how to proceed. We often focus too strongly on the 'urgent and important' field, on the things that have to be dealt with immediately. Ask yourself: When will I deal with the things that are important, but not urgent? When will I take the time to deal with important tasks before they become urgent? This is the field for strategic, long-term decisions.

Another method of organising your time better is attributed to the multimillionaire Warren Buffett. Make a list of everything you want to get done today. Begin with the task at the top of the list, and continue only when you have completed it. When a task has been completed, cross it off the list.

Better late than never. But never late is better.

Fill in the tasks you currently have to deal with.

THE SWOT ANALYSIS

HOW TO FIND THE RIGHT SOLUTION

With SWOT analysis, you evaluate the Strengths, Weaknesses, Opportunities and Threats identified in a project. The technique is based on a Stanford University study from the 1960s which analysed data from Fortune 500 companies. The study found a 35 per cent discrepancy between the companies' objectives and what was actually implemented. The problem was not that the employees were incompetent but that the objectives were too ambiguous. Many employees didn't even know why they were doing what they were doing. SWOT was developed from the results of the study to help those involved in a project to gain a clearer understanding of it.

It is worth taking the time to think about each step of the SWOT analysis rather than just hastily fill it out. How can we emphasise our strengths and compensate for (or cover up) our weaknesses? How can we maximise opportunities? How can we protect ourselves against threats?

What is interesting about SWOT analysis is its versatility: it can be applied to business and personal decisions with equal success.

The things we fear most in organisations – fluctuations, disturbances, imbalances – are the primary sources of creativity.
Margaret J. Wheatley

Think back to a big project in your life and about how you would have filled in a SWOT diagram at the time. Compare that with how you would fill it in today.

THE BCG BOX

HOW TO EVALUATE COSTS AND BENEFITS

In the 1970s, the Boston Consulting Group developed a method for assessing the value of the investments in a company's portfolio. The four-field matrix distinguishes between four different types of investment:

- **Cash cows** have a high market share but a low growth rate. This means they don't cost much but promise high returns. Consultants' verdict: milk them.
- **Stars** have a high market share and a high growth rate. But growth devours money. The hope is that the stars will turn into cash cows. Consultants' verdict: invest.
- **Question marks**, or 'problem children', have high growth potential but a low share of the market. With a lot of (financial) support and cajolement, they can be turned into stars. Consultants' verdict: a tough decision.
- **Dogs** are business units with a low share in a saturated market. Dogs should be held on to only if they have a value other than a financial one (e.g. a vanity project or favour for a friend). Consultants' verdict: liquidate.

The most dangerous words in investing are 'this time it's different'.
Sir John Templeton

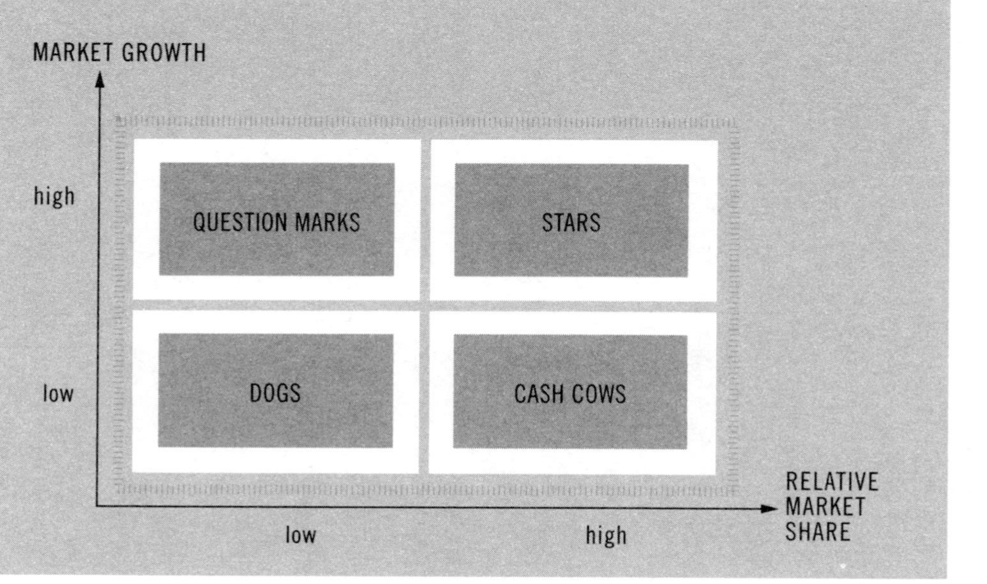

Arrange your financial products, investments or projects in the matrix. The axes indicate growth potential and market share.

THE PROJECT PORTFOLIO MATRIX

HOW TO MAINTAIN AN OVERVIEW

Are you juggling several projects simultaneously? Then you are a 'slasher' (/). The term was coined by the New York author Marci Alboher and describes a growing number of people who cannot give a single answer to the question 'And what do you do for a living?'

Suppose you are a teacher/musician/web designer. The variety may be appealing, but how can you balance all these projects? And how do you ensure a regular income?

To get an overview, you can classify your current projects, both work-related and private, with the help of the project portfolio matrix according to cost and time (see model). Think of costs not only in terms of money but also in terms of resources such as friends involved, energy and psychological stress.

Cost and time are just two examples. You can use whatever parameters are relevant to your situation: for example, the x-axis could be 'How much my project is helping me achieve my overriding objective', and the y-axis 'How much I am learning from this project'. Now position your projects in the matrix in relation to the two axes 'objectives achieved' and 'amount learned'.

HOW TO INTERPRET THE RESULTS

- Reject projects if there is nothing you can learn from them and if they do not correspond to your overriding vision.
- Projects that you can learn from but do not correspond to your vision are interesting but will not help you achieve your objective. Try to change the project so that it serves your vision.

- If a project corresponds to your vision, but you are learning nothing new, look for somebody else to do it for you.
- If you are learning something and achieving your vision, you have hit the jackpot!

The greatest danger for most of us is not that our aim is too high and we miss it, but that it is too low and we reach it. *Michelangelo*

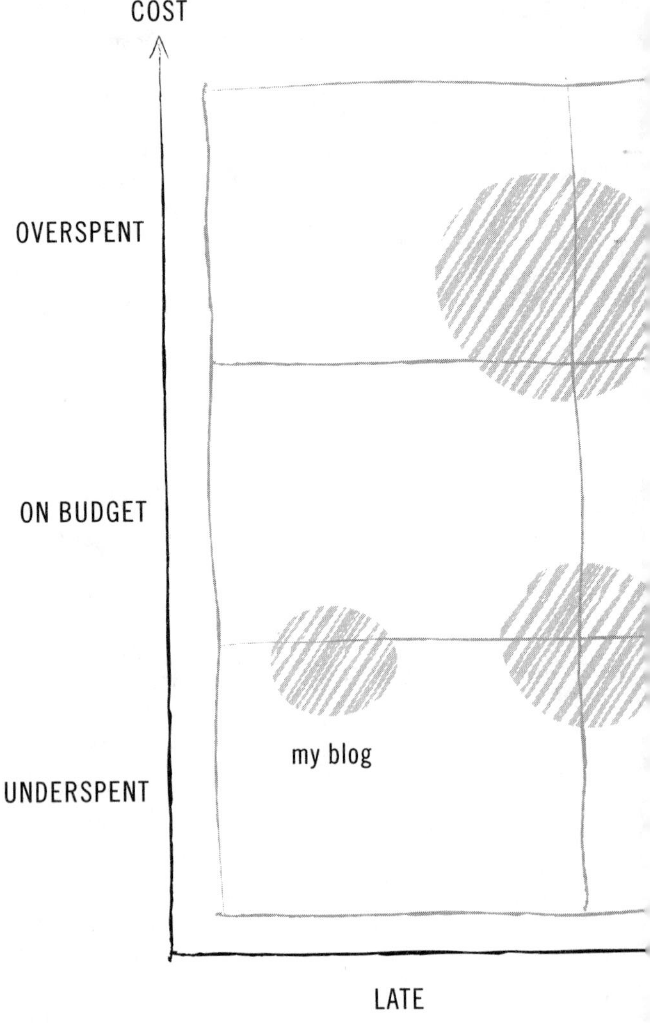

Arrange your current projects in the matrix: are you on budget and on time?

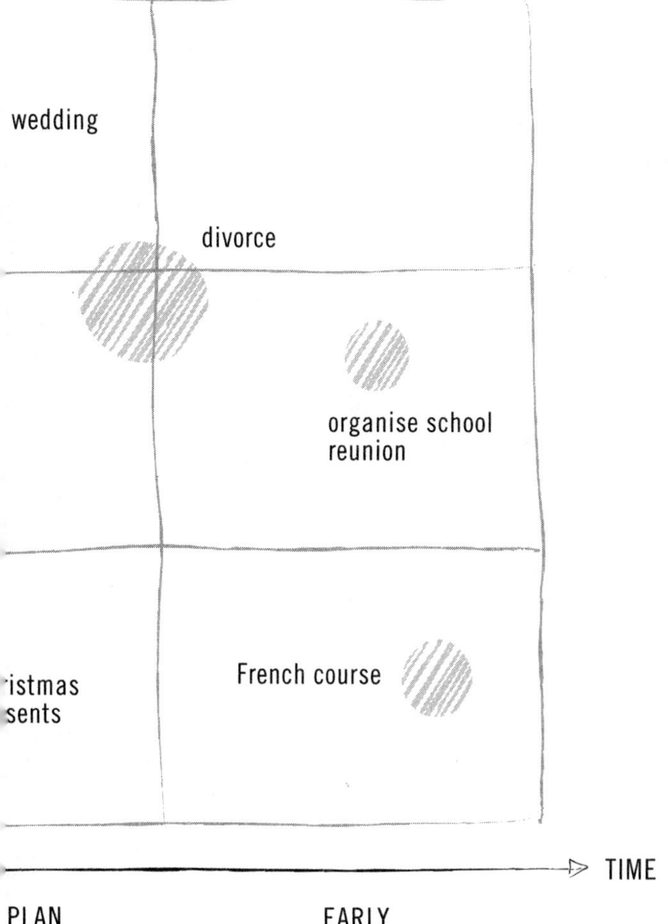

wedding
divorce
organise school reunion
ristmas
sents
French course
TIME
PLAN
EARLY

THE JOHN WHITMORE MODEL

AM I PURSUING THE RIGHT GOAL?

If you set yourself goals, you should distinguish between final goals and performance goals. A final goal might be 'I want to run a marathon'; a performance goal helps you achieve this aim, for example 'I will go jogging for thirty minutes every morning'.

Write down your goal on paper and check, step by step, whether it correlates with the fourteen requirements in the model.

A few things to note: if a goal is unattainable, there is no hope, and if it is not challenging it will not motivate you. If the fourteen steps are too complicated for you, keep in mind the following ground rule when establishing your goal:

KISS – Keep It Simple, Stupid!

Everything should be made as simple as possible. But no simpler.
Albert Einstein

➥See also: Flow model (p.46)

S	SPECIFIC	THE RIGHT GOAL		C	CHALLENGING
M	MEASURABLE	P	POSITIVELY STATED	L	LEGAL
A	ATTAINABLE	U	UNDERSTOOD	E	ENVIRONMENTALLY SOUND
R	REALISTIC	R	RELEVANT	A	AGREED
T	TIME PHASED	E	ETHICAL	R	RECORDED

Once you have established a goal, check whether it correlates with these fourteen requirements.

THE RUBBER BAND MODEL

HOW TO DEAL WITH A DILEMMA

Is this a situation you are familiar with? A friend, colleague or client needs to make a decision that could irrevocably alter their future: for example to change career, move to another city or take early retirement. The arguments for and against are evenly balanced. How can you help them out of their dilemma?

Copy out the rubber band model, and ask the person to ask themselves: What is holding me? What is pulling me?

At first glance the method seems to be a simple variation of the conventional question 'What are the pros and cons?' The difference is that 'What is holding me?' and 'What is pulling me?' are positive questions and reflect a situation with two attractive alternatives.

A peacefulness follows any decision, even the wrong one.
Rita Mae Brown

→See also: SWOT analysis (p.12)

WHAT IS HOLDING YOU?
WHAT IS PULLING YOU?

If you have to decide between two good options, ask yourself what is holding you, and what is pulling you.

THE FEEDBACK MODEL

DEALING WITH OTHER PEOPLE'S COMPLIMENTS AND CRITICISMS

Feedback is one of the most difficult and sensitive processes in groups. It is easy to hurt people with criticism, but false compliments are also unhelpful. Compliments often make us too complacent, while criticism damages our self-esteem and can lead us to make unwise choices.

The one-dimensional question 'What did you find good, what did you find bad?' is therefore not necessarily helpful. In terms of what can be learned from feedback, it is better to ask yourself 'What can I do with this criticism?' In other words, see what can stay as it is, and what needs to change (but may have been good up till now).

It is not only about establishing what has not succeeded, it is also about deciding whether and how to react. The model will help you to categorise the feedback you receive in order to clearly establish a plan of action.

It is also important to ask yourself honestly: 'Which success or failure was in fact due to luck?' Were you the winner of a match because the ball found its way into the net purely by chance? Do you really deserve this compliment?

Pay attention to your thoughts, because they become words.
Pay attention to your words, because they become actions.
Pay attention to your actions, because they become habits.
Pay attention to your habits, because they become your character.
Pay attention to your character, because it is your fate.
From the Talmud

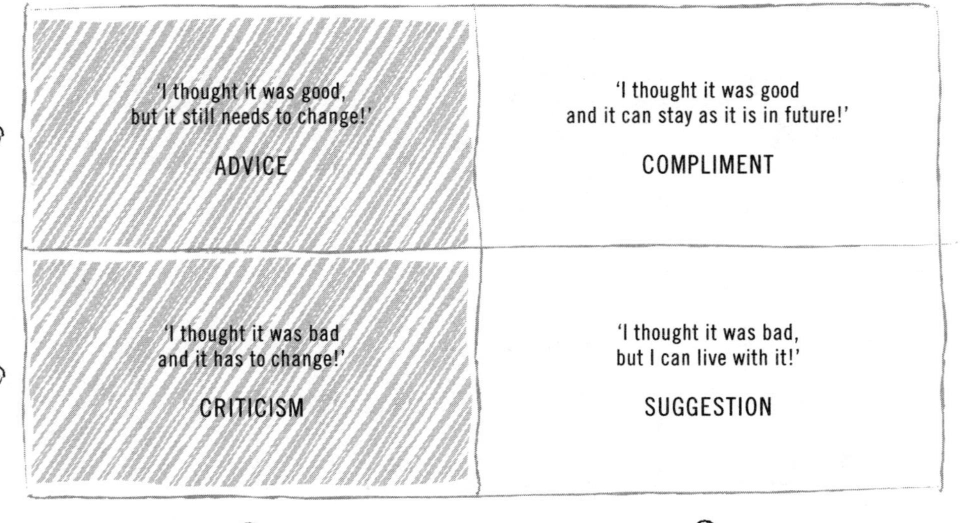

‘I thought it was good,
but it still needs to change!’
ADVICE
‘I thought it was good
and it can stay as it is in future!’
COMPLIMENT
‘I thought it was bad
and it has to change!’
CRITICISM
‘I thought it was bad,
but I can live with it!’
SUGGESTION

Arrange the feedback you have received in the matrix. What advice do you want to follow? Which criticisms prompt you to take action? Which suggestions can you ignore?

THE FAMILY TREE MODEL

THE CONTACTS YOU SHOULD MAINTAIN

This model is based on the premise that humans are fundamentally social, interactive beings. Brand loyalty can be understood as a person's attachment to a brand or product, and that person's desire to tell others about it. Conventional models for determining brand loyalty often serve as a justification of (often imprudent) expenditure or of decisions that have already been made rather than as an objective evaluation of strategies.

A simpler and more constructive starting point for determining brand loyalty is to find out what your customers think about your product. Instead of a complex questionnaire, in this model the customer is asked a single question: 'Who recommended this product to you, and who would you recommend it to?' Three groups of respondents can be defined based on the answers: promoters, passive satisfied customers and critics. The ratio of promoters to critics is the barometer of success.

Draw a client or portfolio structure in the shape of a family tree. Now you will see how or through whom a client became a client.

HELP WITH INTERPRETATION

The more family trees you have to draw, the more diverse your customer structure or portfolio. Boughs with more branches require more maintenance. They represent a risk of over-concentration and can easily break.

You don't have customers? Then think about how your circle of friends and acquaintances is structured. Through whom did you meet most of your friends? Are you still friends with this person?

→See also: Network target model (p.80)

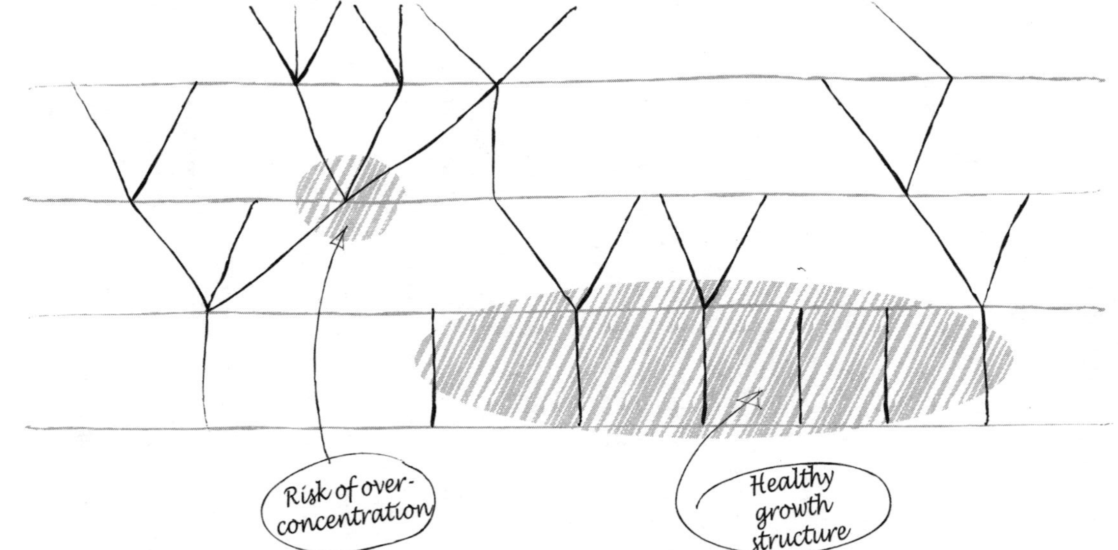

Draw the family tree of your friends and acquaintances: through whom do you know your friends? Or draw the tree of your clients: through whom have you reached most of your customers?

THE MORPHOLOGICAL BOX AND SCAMPER

WHY YOU HAVE TO BE STRUCTURED TO BE CREATIVE

Innovation can mean doing something completely new, but it can also mean making a new combination of things that already exist. But how is this achieved?

The concept of morphology stems from the study of biological structures and configurations. In the 1930s, the Swiss physicist Fritz Zwicky at the Institute of Technology in California developed a problem-solving method using what he called morphological boxes, in which a new entity is developed by combining the attributes of a variety of existing entities. This method, which was initially applied by Zwicky to jet engine technology, also began to be used in marketing strategies and the development of new ideas.

HOW IT WORKS

For the development of a new car, for example, all the relevant parameters (e.g. vehicle type, target group) are noted, and as many attributes as possible are ascribed to each parameter. This requires expertise as well as imagination, as the aim is to create something new out of something that already exists. The result in this case is a two-dimensional table (although a morphological box can have up to four dimensions).

The next stage requires brainstorming: the car has to be an SUV, say, but it also needs to be energy-efficient and inexpensive to manufacture. Which attributes match these requirements? Connect your chosen attributes with a line. This new configuration of attributes can form the basis for an evaluation of your desired car.

Besides the morphological boxes, the SCAMPER checklist developed by Bob Eberle will also help you to reconfigure an existing idea or product. The following seven key questions are drawn from a questionnaire developed by Alex Osborn, founder of the advertising agency BBDO:

- **Substitute?** Substitute people, components, materials.
- **Combine?** Combine with other functions or things.
- **Adapt?** Adapt functions or visual appearance.
- **Modify?** Modify the size, shape, texture or acoustics.
- **Put to other use?** Other, new, combined uses.
- **Eliminate?** Reduce, simplify, eliminate anything superfluous.
- **Reverse?** Use conversely, invert, reverse.

The task is not so much *to see what no one has yet seen*, but to think what nobody yet has thought about that which everybody sees. *Arthur Schopenhauer*

↬See also: Thinking outside the box (p.92)

CONFIGURATION / PARAMETERS	CONFIGURATION 1	CONFIGUR
DESIGN (FRONT VIEW)	aggressive	angular (new edg
PERFORMANCE, ENGINE	petrol 100–200 hp	petrol 200–300
SEATS/ROOM	2	4
VEHICLE TYPE	limousine	mini-van
STYLE	confident	cool
FEATURES, MARKETING ASSETS	DVD-player (cooperation with Blockbuster)	integrate music do from onli stores
TARGET GROUP	HNWIs High Net Worth Individuals	DINKs Double In No Kids

URATION 3	CONFIGURATION 4	CONFIGURATION 5	CONFIGURATION 6
	flowing	sporty	athletic
l	hybrid	hydrogen	electric
	6	6+	6+ incl. fully reclinable seat
	estate	coupe	pick-up
dly	cheeky	'French'	'American'
ner for uning	Partnership with National Rail for inter-city services	new paintwork of choice every year	fridge, even kitchenette
IPIEs er Radical, rd Moving e	LOHAS Lifestyle Of Health And Sustainability	WOOPIEs Well Off Older People	MILKIEs Modest Introverted Luxury Keeper

THE *ESQUIRE* GIFT MODEL

HOW MUCH TO SPEND ON GIFTS

Gift-giving is something of a minefield. A cheap or impersonal gift can make the recipient feel undervalued, and create an awkward situation for both giver and receiver. This little model from *Esquire* magazine has two axes:

- How long have you known the person to whom you are giving the gift?
- How much money should you spend on the gift?

TWO RULES OF THUMB

Being generous beats being miserly (don't be misled by the sentence 'That really wasn't necessary').

Buy something that you would be pleased to receive as a gift yourself.

I have the simplest tastes. I am always satisfied with the best.
Oscar Wilde

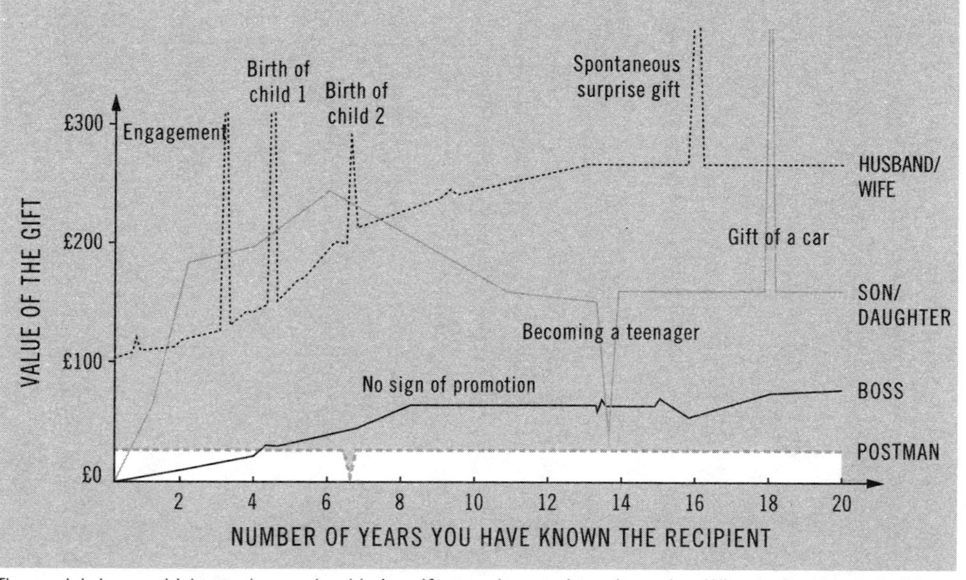

The model shows which people you should give gifts to, when, and to what value. What is the most valuable gift you have ever given – and received?

THE CONSEQUENCES MODEL

WHY IT IS IMPORTANT TO MAKE DECISIONS PROMPTLY

We are often forced to make decisions based on limited or ambiguous information. At the beginning of a project, for example, when the finer details have yet to be clarified, we need to be bold in our decision-making – particularly because these early decisions have the most far-reaching consequences. Towards the end of a project we know more and have fewer doubts, but by then there is no longer anything fundamental to decide.

The most important question, then, is how we can bridge the chasm between doubt and decision.

Beware! We often defer decisions because we have doubts. But not making a decision is a decision in itself. If you delay a resolution it is often an unconscious decision, one that you do not communicate. This leads to uncertainty in a team. So if you want to make a decision later, be sure to communicate this clearly.

With this model, the Danish organisation theorists Kristian Kreiner and Søren Christensen encourage us to be courageous, and make decisions based on minimal information.

I'd rather regret the things I have done than the things that I haven't. *Lucille Ball*

➥See also: Eisenhower matrix (p.10)

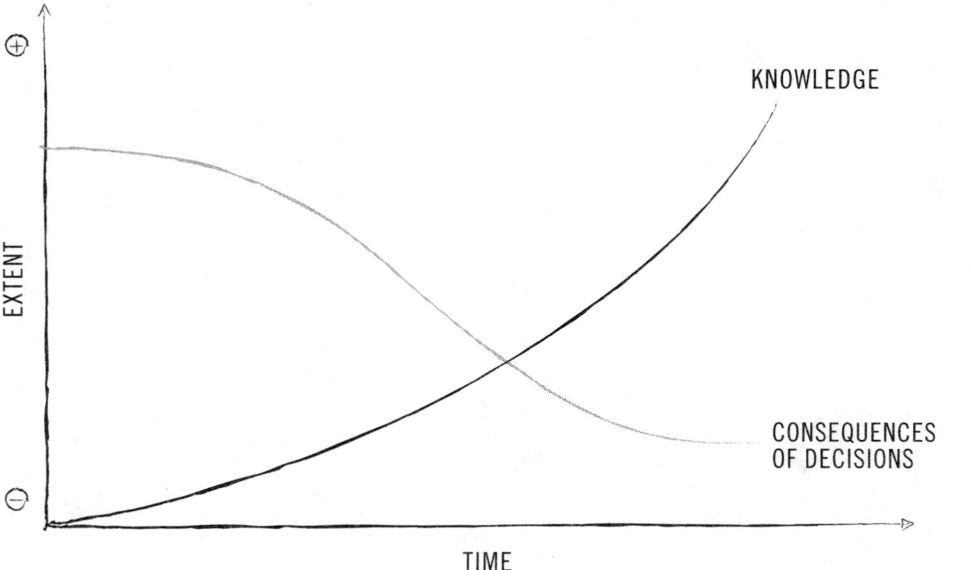

The model shows how the extent of the consequences of your decisions relates to the extent of your knowledge.

THE CONFLICT RESOLUTION MODEL

HOW TO RESOLVE A CONFLICT ELEGANTLY

Psychologists agree that conflicts have to be dealt with in order to prevent deadlock and recrimination and restore stability and communication. The question is, how? In principle there are six different ways of dealing with a conflict situation: escape, fight, give up, evade responsibility, compromise or reach a consensus.

1. **Escape**. Escaping is the same as avoiding. The conflict is not dealt with, and the situation remains the same. It can be assumed that neither side will gain anything. This is a lose–lose situation.

2. **Fight**. Those who deal with a conflict aggressively have only one aim: to win. But winning alone is not enough, as somebody also has to lose. This approach is about conquering the opponent, and asserting one's own position in the face of resistance from others. The result is a win–lose situation.

3. **Give up**. Those who give up their own position in a conflict solve it by retreating, i.e. they lose. The result is a lose–win situation.

4. **Evade responsibility**. Those who feel overwhelmed by a conflict often delegate the decision – and thus also the confrontation – to another authority, usually a higher one. This authority solves the conflict for them, but not necessarily wisely, and not necessarily in the delegator's interest. There is a risk that the parties on both sides of the conflict will lose (lose–lose situation).

5. **Compromise**. Depending on how it is perceived, a compromise

is a solution acceptable to both parties. It is often felt that although the solution isn't ideal, it is reasonable in the circumstances (win–lose/win–lose).

6. **Reach a consensus**. A consensus is based on a new solution that has been developed by both parties. In contrast to a compromise, it is a win–win situation for both parties, because nobody has to back down. Instead, both parties develop a 'third way' together.

Our failures are due not to the defeats we suffer but to the conflicts we don't participate in.
Graffiti on a youth centre in Bern, Switzerland

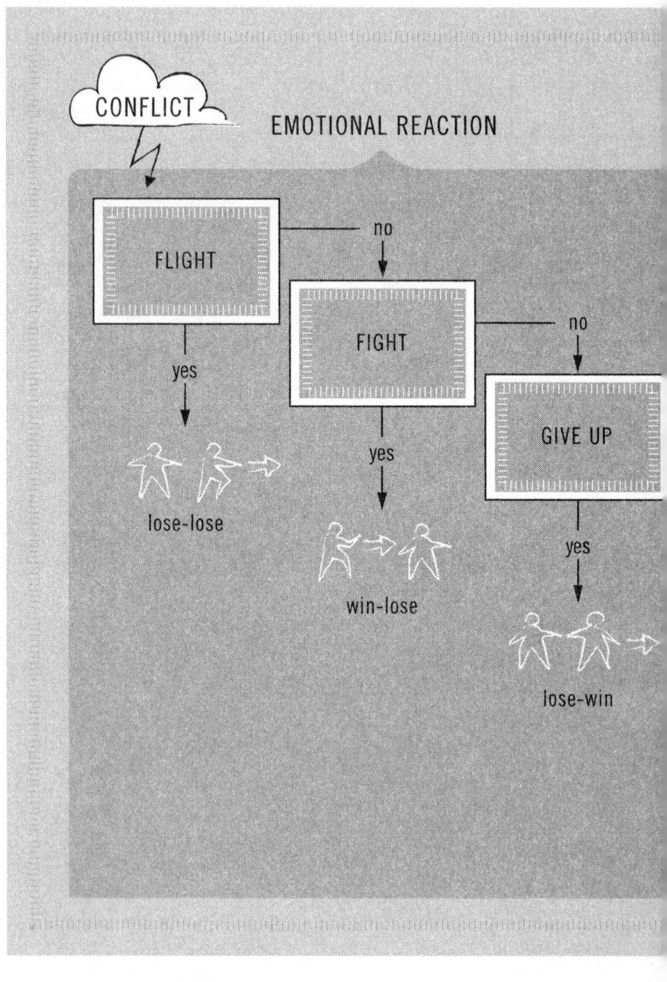

This model shows the six typical reactions to a conflict. What conflict type are you? What type is your adversary?

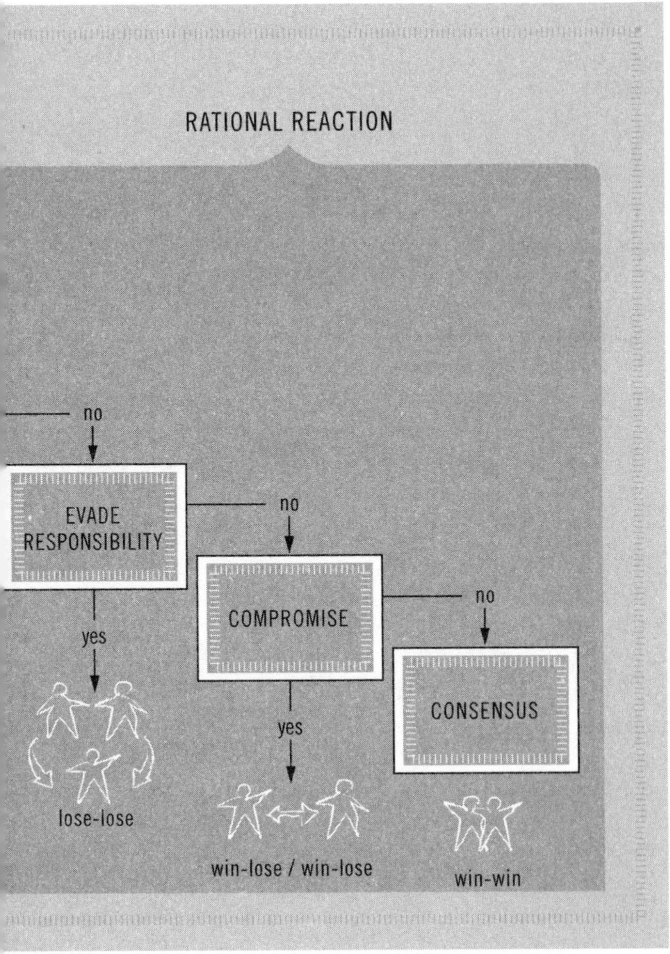

RATIONAL REACTION

no

EVADE RESPONSIBILITY

no

yes

COMPROMISE

no

lose-lose

yes

CONSENSUS

win-lose / win-lose

win-win

THE CROSSROADS MODEL

SO WHAT NEXT?

We all have times in our lives when we find ourselves at a crossroads, and ask ourselves: where now? The crossroads model is inspired by *The Personal Compass*, developed by San Francisco consulting agency The Grove, and helps you to find your direction in life. Fill in the model on the basis of the following questions:

WHERE HAVE YOU COME FROM?

How have you become who you are? What have been the main decisions, events and obstacles in your life, and who were your main influences? Think about your education, your home, where you grew up. And make a note of keywords that strike you as important.

WHAT IS REALLY IMPORTANT TO YOU?

Write down the first three things that come into your head. You don't have to go into detail or be specific. What are your values? What do you believe in? Which principles are important to you? When everything fails, what remains?

WHICH PEOPLE ARE IMPORTANT TO YOU?

Here you should think of people whose opinions you value, and who influence your decisions, as well as those who are affected by your decisions. Think also about the people you like and those you fear.

WHAT IS HINDERING YOU?

What aspects of your life prevent you from thinking about the really important things? Which deadlines do you have in your head, and what is hindering you? What do you have to do, and when?

WHAT ARE YOU AFRAID OF?

List the things, circumstances or people that cause you worry and rob you of your strength.

Look at your notes. What's missing? What issues have arisen? Do the keywords you've written down tell the story of how you became who you are today? If necessary, jot down more keywords and questions. Now look at the roads that lie ahead of you. We have given six examples. Imagine each one:

1. The road that beckons – what have you always wanted to try?
2. The road that I imagine in my wildest dreams, regardless of whether it is achievable or not – what do you dream of?
3. The road that seems most sensible to me, the one that people whose opinion I value would suggest to me.
4. The road not travelled – one you have never considered before.
5. The road I have already been down.
6. The road back, to a place you once felt safe.

You decide.

When was the last time you did something for the first time?

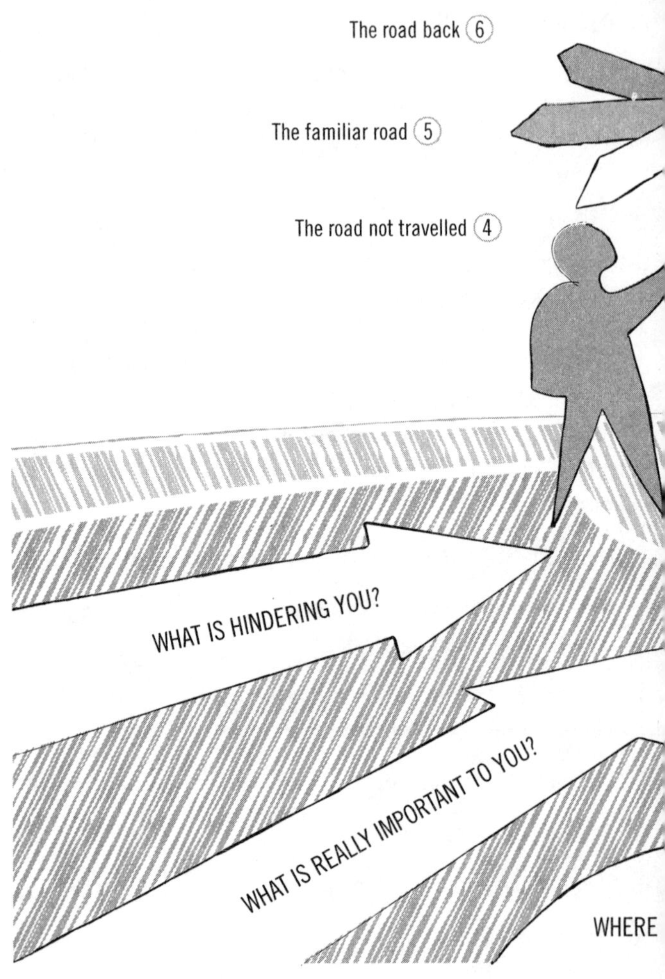

Answer the questions by yourself or together with a good friend. Then imagine the road that you could take.

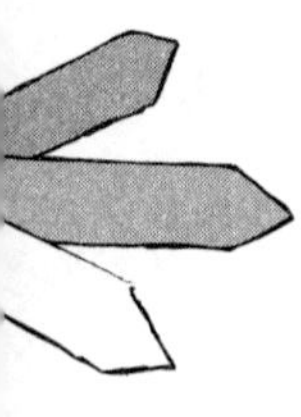

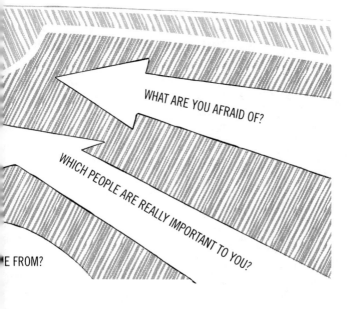

WHAT ARE YOU AFRAID OF?

WHICH PEOPLE ARE REALLY IMPORTANT TO YOU?

E FROM?

HOW TO UNDERSTAND YOURSELF BETTER

THE FLOW MODEL

WHAT MAKES YOU HAPPY?

Over two thousand years ago, Aristotle came to the unsurprising conclusion that what a person wants above all is to be happy. In 1961, the US psychologist Mihaly Csikszentmihalyi wrote: 'While happiness itself is sought for its own sake, every other goal – health, beauty, money or power – is valued only because we expect that it will make us happy.' Csikszentmihalyi looked for a term that described the state of feeling happy. He called it 'flow.' But when are we 'in the flow'?

After interviewing over a thousand people about what made them happy, he found that all the responses had five things in common. Happiness, or 'flow', occurs when we are:

- intensely focused on an activity
- of our own choosing, that is
- neither under-challenging (boreout) nor over-challenging (burnout), that has
- a clear objective, and that receives
- immediate feedback.

Csikszentmihalyi discovered that people who are 'in the flow' not only feel a profound sense of satisfaction, they also lose track of time and forget themselves completely because they are so immersed in what they are doing. Musicians, athletes, actors, doctors and artists describe how they are happiest when they are absorbed in an often exhausting activity – totally contradicting the commonly held view that happiness has to do with relaxation.

What is preventing you from being happy?

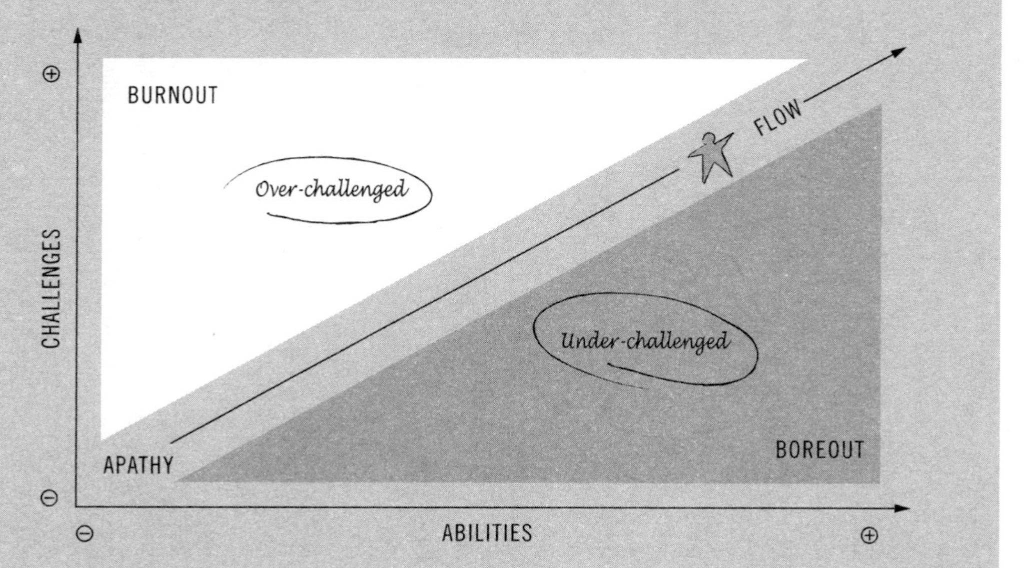

The model has two axes: the level of the challenge, and the level of your abilities. On the graph, write down the last three challenges you have faced, and how you felt about them.

THE JOHARI WINDOW

WHAT OTHERS KNOW ABOUT YOU

We cannot 'grasp' our own personality, but we can be aware of what part of our personality we reveal to the outside world. The Johari window ('Johari' is derived from the first syllables of the first names of its inventors, Joseph Luft and Harry Ingham) is one of the most interesting models for describing human interaction. A four-paned 'window' divides personal awareness into four different types:

A. This quadrant describes characteristics and experiences that we are aware of ourselves and that we like to tell others about.

B. This 'hidden' quadrant describes things that we know about ourselves but choose not reveal to others. It decreases in size the more we build up a trusting relationship with others.

C. There are things that we do not know about ourselves but that others can see clearly. And there are things that we think we are expressing clearly, but which others interpret completely differently. In this quadrant, feedback can be enlightening but also hurtful.

D. There are aspects of ourselves that are hidden from ourselves as well as others. We are more complex and multifaceted than we think. From time to time something unknown rises to the surface from our unconscious – for example in a dream.

Choose adjectives (fun, unreliable, etc.) that you think describe you well. Then let others (friends, colleagues) choose adjectives to describe you. The adjectives are then entered in the appropriate panes of the window.

Try this exercise with your partner. Are there things about your partner that you wished you had never discovered? And what do you wish you didn't know about yourself?

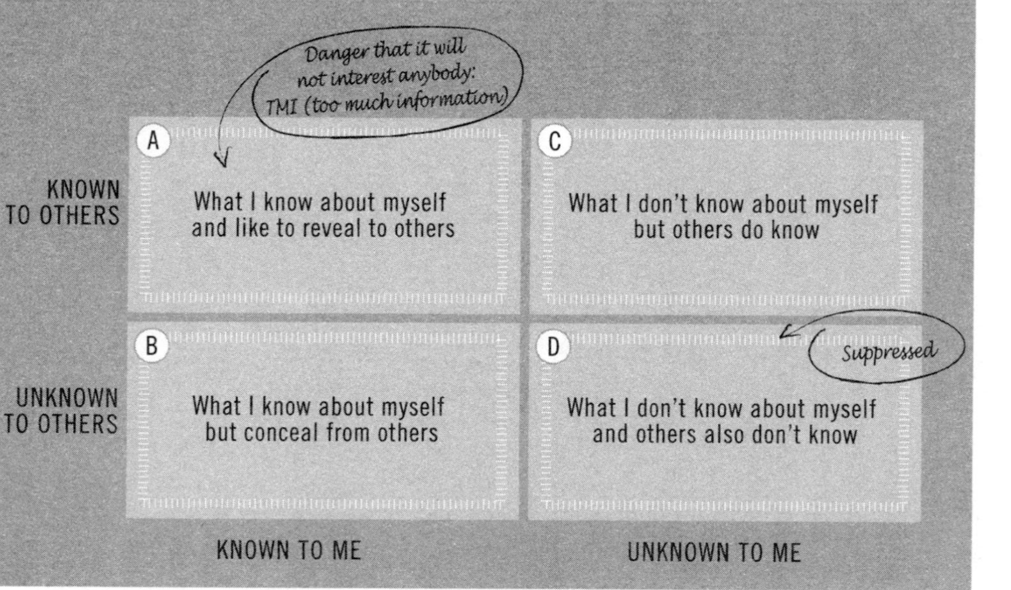

What do others know about you that you don't know yourself? The Johari window provides a model of personal awareness.

THE COGNITIVE DISSONANCE MODEL

WHY PEOPLE SMOKE WHEN THEY KNOW IT'S UNHEALTHY

There is often a big gap between what we think and what we do: when we do something despite knowing it to be immoral, wrong or stupid, we have a bad conscience. The psychologist Leon Festinger used the term 'cognitive dissonance' to describe our state of mind when our actions are not consistent with our beliefs – for example when we smack a child, even though we condemn violence against children.

But why do we find it so difficult to recognise our mistakes? Why do we even go as far as defending our actions when we are confronted with their shortcomings? Rather than asking for forgiveness, we embark on one of the more unlikeable human attributes: self-justification. This acts as a protective mechanism that enables us to sleep at night and frees us from self-doubt. We see only what we want to see, and ignore everything that contradicts our view. We look for arguments that reinforce our position.

But how can we overcome this dissonance? Either by changing our behaviour or our attitude.

A great nation is like a great man: when he makes a mistake, he realises it. Having realised it, he admits it. Having admitted it, he corrects it. He considers those who point out his faults as his most benevolent teachers. *Lao Zi*

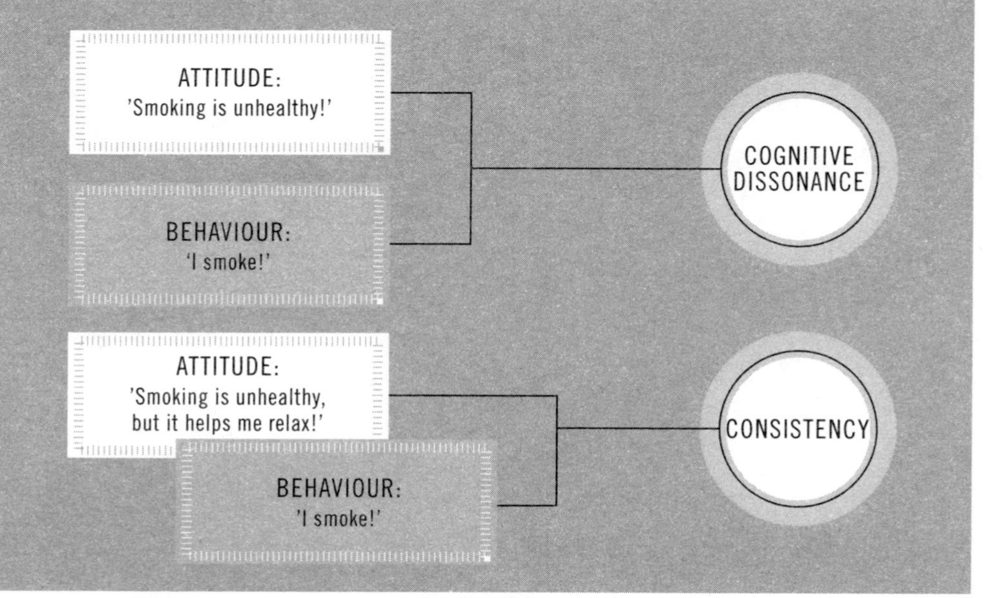

When were you last aware of a cognitive dissonance in yourself? And when in your partner?

THE MUSIC MATRIX

WHAT YOUR TASTE IN MUSIC SAYS ABOUT YOU

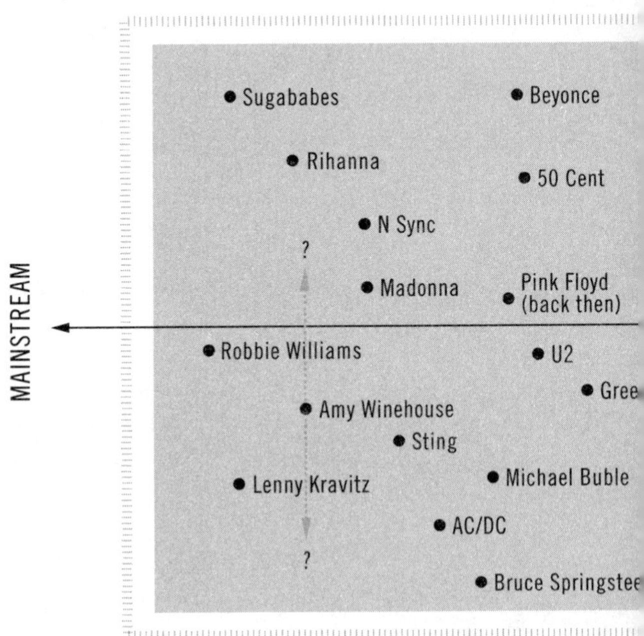

Insert your favourite bands in the matrix.

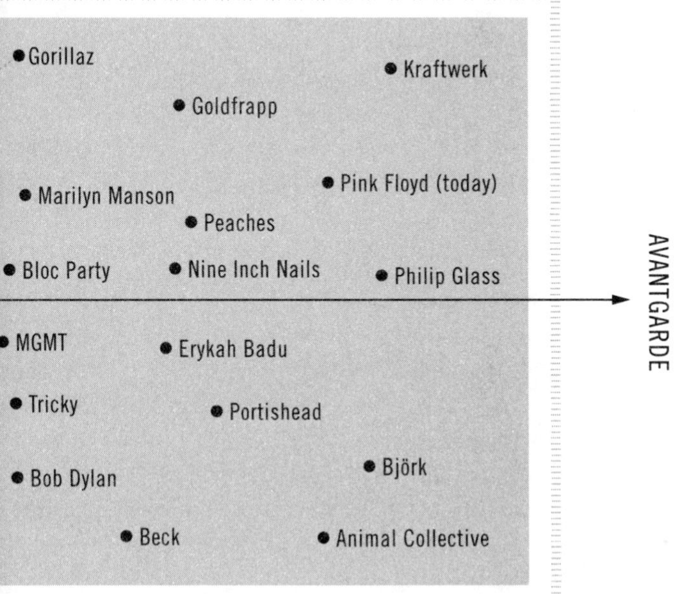
Gorillaz
Kraftwerk
Goldfrapp
Pink Floyd (today)
Marilyn Manson
Peaches
Bloc Party
Nine Inch Nails
Philip Glass
AVANTGARDE
MGMT
Erykah Badu
Tricky
Portishead
Björk
Bob Dylan
Beck
Animal Collective

AUTHENTIC

THE UNIMAGINABLE MODEL

WHAT DO YOU BELIEVE IN THAT YOU CANNOT PROVE?

Models explain how everything is connected, how we should act and what we should and should not do. But do they prevent us from seeing things for what they really are?

As early as the eighteenth century, Adam Smith warned against being carried away by a love of abstract systems, and two centuries later Albert Einstein received a Nobel Prize for recognising that models and 'logical' systems are ultimately a matter of faith. The historian of science and philosopher Thomas Kuhn argued that science usually just works towards corroborating its models, and reacts with ignorance when – as is often the case – the models do not correspond to reality. This insight may not have earned him a Nobel Prize, but he did land himself a professorship at an elite university.

We often believe so strongly in models that they take on the status of reality. A good example of this is the ontological proof of the existence of God, which Kant explored in his philosophy. He maintained that if we are able to imagine a being as perfect as God, then he must exist. Ways in which we blindly accept models as 'reality' can also be found in our everyday lives: for example, if we are told that humankind is full of greed and egoism, this model of behaviour may be internalised and (unconsciously) imitated.

I hate reality but it's still the best place to get a good steak.
Woody Allen

➥See also: Black box model (p.118), The world's next top model (p.148)

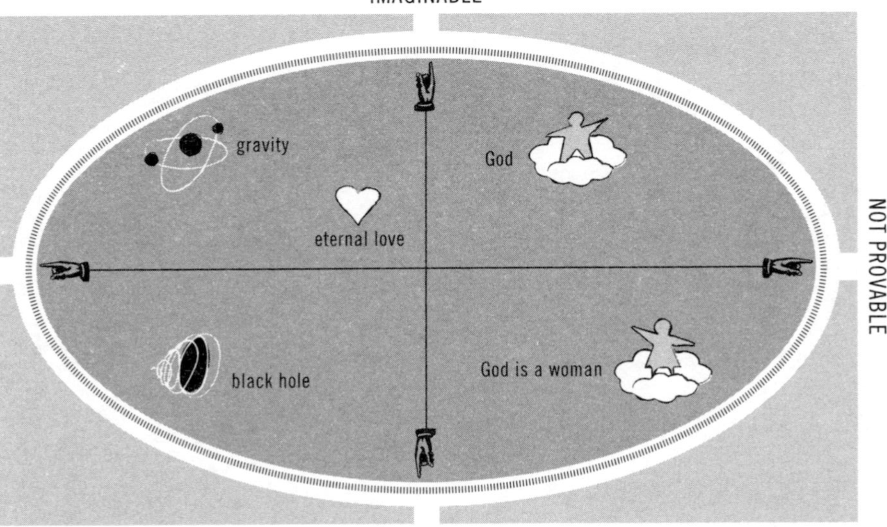

What do you believe in, despite not understanding the evidence? And what do you believe in despite having no evidence to support it?

THE UFFE ELBÆK MODEL

HOW TO GET TO KNOW YOURSELF

If you want gain a general understanding of yourself and others, Uffe Elbæk's public opinion barometer is a good starting point. It reveals behavioural traits and tendencies.

You should bear in mind that you are always subject to four different perspectives:

- how you see yourself
- how you would like to see yourself
- how others see you
- how others would like to see you

PROCEED AS FOLLOWS

- Without taking time to think about it, decide the following on a scale of one to ten. How much of a team person are you, and how much of an individualist? Do you pay more attention to content or to form? What is more important to you: the body or the mind? Do you feel more global than local? Use a pen to connect the lines.
- Now take a different coloured pen to mark on the scale how you would like to see yourself.
- Define your own axes (rich–poor, happy–sad, extroverted–introverted).

Beware! You are only creating a snapshot. And note that the sum of an axis should always be ten (you cannot be ten points local and ten points global).

What is preventing you from being the way you would like to be?

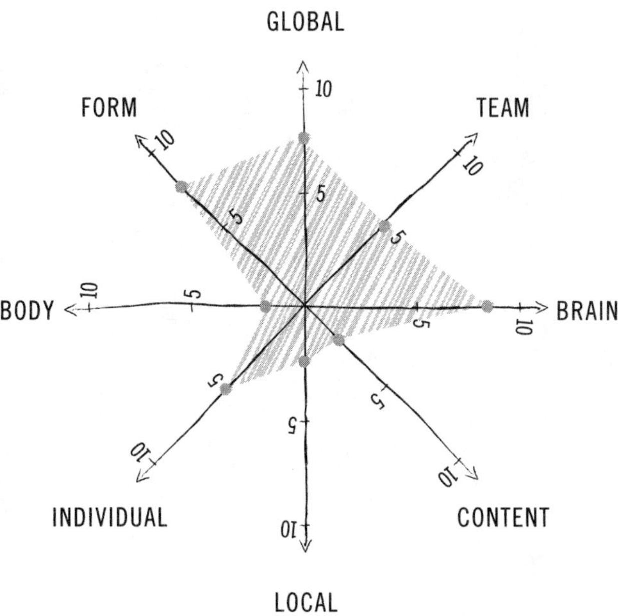

Fill in the model for yourself. Then ask your partner or a good friend to fill it in for you. Compare the results.

THE FASHION MODEL

HOW WE DRESS

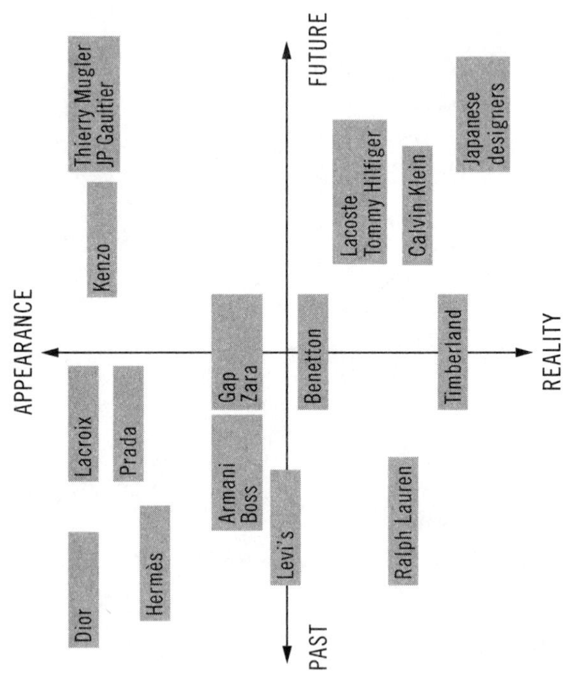

The writer Eric Sommier created this model in which he positions well-known clothing brands.

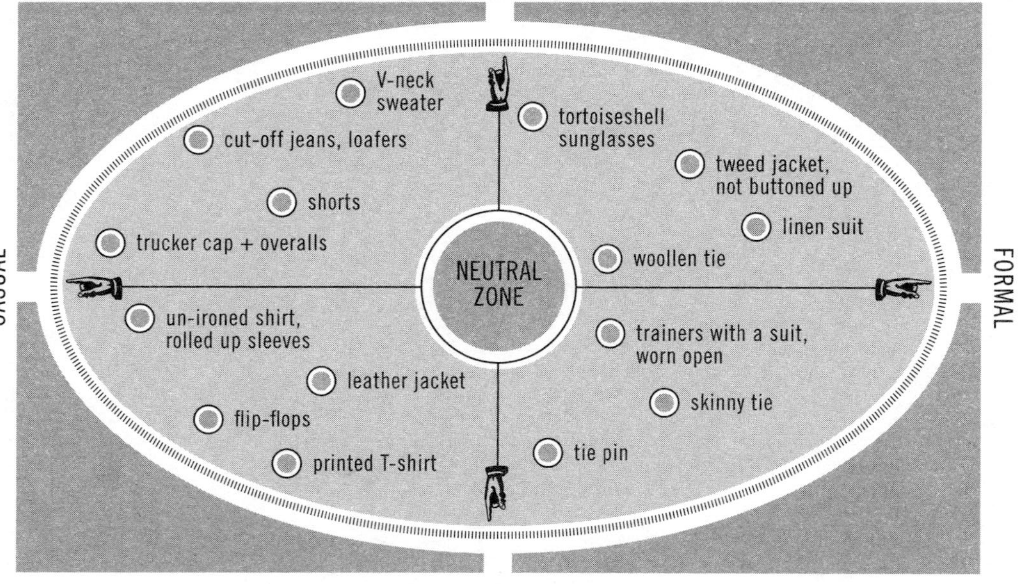

The art of dressing without dressing up.

THE ENERGY MODEL

ARE YOU LIVING IN THE HERE AND NOW?

It is always said that we should live 'in the here and now.' But why? The Swiss author Pascal Mercier says this: 'It is an error, a nonsensical act of violence, to concentrate on the here and now with the conviction of thus grasping the essential. What matters is to move surely and calmly, with the appropriate humour and the appropriate melancholy in the temporally and spatially internal landscape that we are.'

Here is a non-judgemental question: how much of your time do you spend thinking about the past, how much about the here and now, and how much about the future? Or to put it another way, how often do you think, wistfully or thankfully, about what has been? How often do you have the feeling that you are really concentrating on what you are doing at a particular moment? How often do you imagine what the future may hold, and how often do you worry about what lies ahead of you?

The three examples shown in the model on the right can also represent cultural values: memory-driven, in nostalgic Europe; dream-driven, in the USA, the 'land of opportunity'; and reality-driven, in industrious Asia.

You can't change the past. But you can ruin the present by worrying about the future.

➥See also: Crossroads model (p.40)

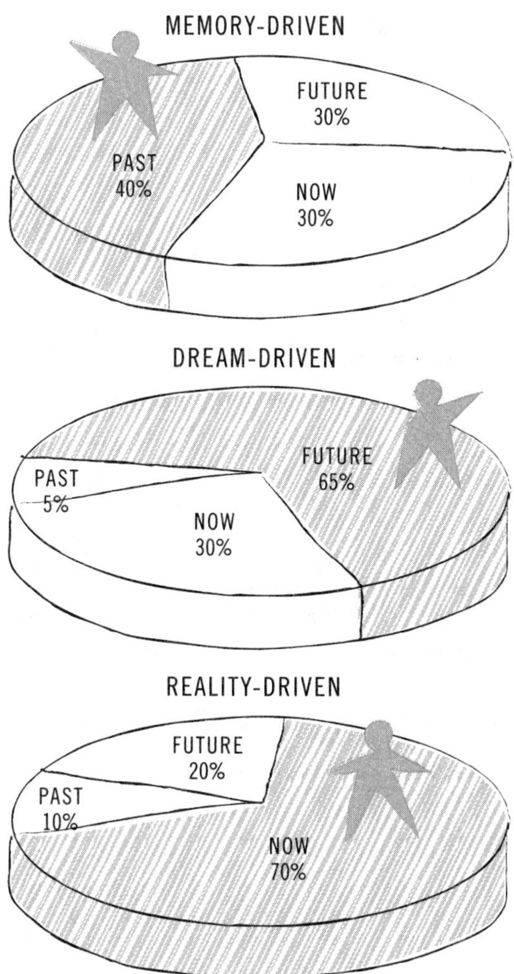

Fill in how much time you spend in the past, present and future.

THE SUPERMEMO MODEL

HOW TO REMEMBER EVERYTHING YOU HAVE EVER LEARNED

Long-term memory has two components: retrievability and stability. Retrievability determines how easily we remember something, and depends on how near the surface of our consciousness the information is 'swimming'. Stability, on the other hand, is to do with how deeply information is anchored in our brains. Some memories have a high level of stability but a low level of retrievability. Try to recall one of your old phone numbers – you probably won't be able to. But if you see the number in front of you, you will recognise it immediately.

Imagine that you are learning Chinese. You have learned a word and memorised it. Without practice, over time it will become increasingly difficult to remember. The amount of time it takes for you to forget it completely can be calculated, and ideally you should be reminded of the word precisely when you are in the process of forgetting it. The more often you are reminded of the word, the longer you will remember it for. This learning programme is called SuperMemo and was developed by the Polish researcher Piotr Woźniak.

It's not what you know, it's what you remember. *Jan Cox*

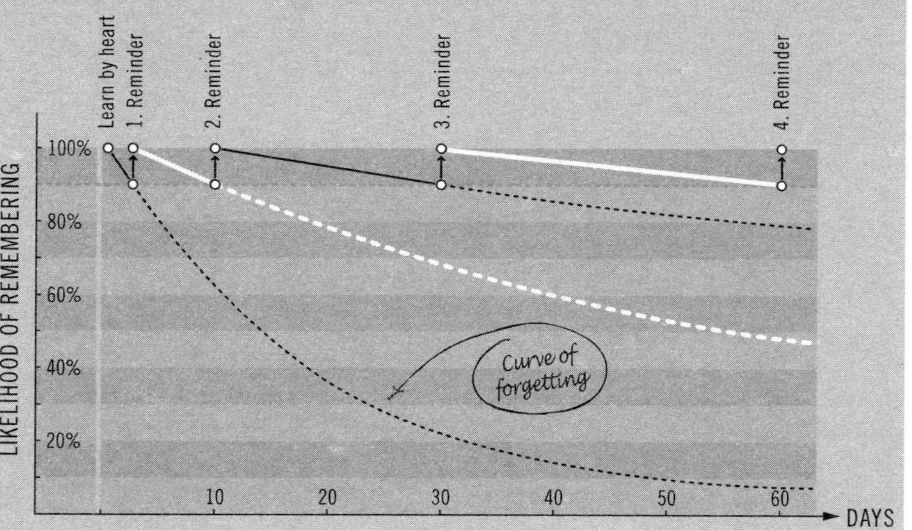

After learning something, you should ideally refresh your memory of it at the following intervals: one, ten, thirty and sixty days afterwards.

THE POLITICAL COMPASS

WHAT POLITICAL PARTIES STAND FOR

Although we still tend to think of politics in terms of 'left' and 'right' this polarisation is too simplistic to describe today's complex political landscape. Traditionally at opposite ends of the political spectrum, Labour and Conservative have moved so close together in terms of shared economic and social policies, that there is little left to distinguish them. Traditional definitions can also be misleading. Its position on race and nationalism means that the BNP is generally regarded as radically right-wing, yet it is far to the left even of Labour when it comes to some social issues like health and housing.

The clear-cut political divisions of the past may have become blurred, but there are models for measuring the views and attitudes of voters. One of the most famous of these tools is called the political compass. You can plot your political position on this model, the axes of which are left–right and liberal–authoritarian.

Note that the left–right axis relates not to political orientation in the traditional sense, but to economic policy: left = nationalisation, right = privatisation. The liberal–authoritarian axis relates to individual rights: liberal = all rights lie with the individual, authoritarian = the state has a high degree of control over its citizens.

Always radical, never consistent. *Walter Benjamin*

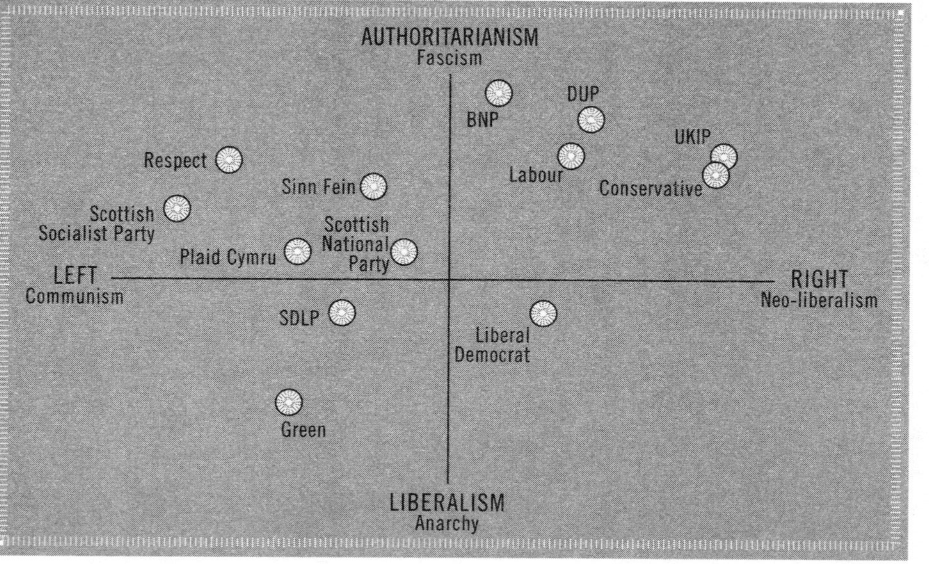

Analysis of the UK political landscape at the time of the 2010 general election by politicalcompass.org.
Ask yourself where you stand. Where did you stand ten years ago?

THE PERSONAL PERFORMANCE MODEL

HOW TO RECOGNISE WHETHER YOU SHOULD CHANGE YOUR JOB

Many people are unhappy in their jobs. But how can job dissatisfaction be measured? This model will help you to evaluate your job situation.

Every evening for three weeks, ask yourself the following three questions, and insert your answers in the model on a scale of one ('doesn't apply at all') to ten ('totally applies'):

- **Have to.** To what extent are my current tasks being imposed on me or demanded of me?
- **Able to.** To what extent do my tasks match my abilities?
- **Want to.** To what extent does my current task correspond to what I really want?

After three weeks, analyse the shapes of the different 'sails'. If you are 'moving', then your job offers you variety. If the shape of the sail is always the same, then ask yourself the following:

- What do you want?
- Are you able to do what you want?
- What are you able to do?
- Do you want what you are able to do?

If you can't do something, you have to work at it.

→See also: Flow model (p.46), Rubber band model (p.22)

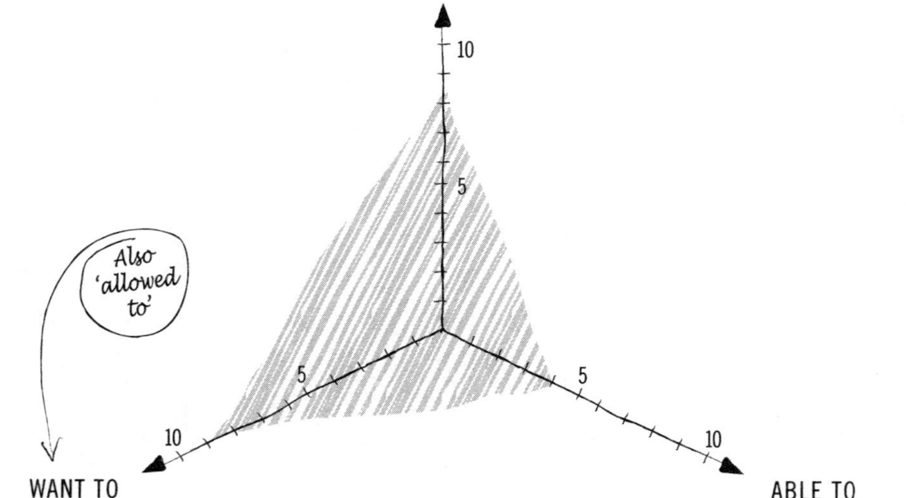

To what extent are your current tasks being imposed on you? To what extent do they match your abilities, and to what extent do they correspond to what you want?

THE MAKING-OF MODEL

TO DETERMINE YOUR FUTURE, FIRST UNDERSTAND YOUR PAST

When it comes to strategic decisions, we usually focus on the future. Our dreams are acted out in the future, and our hopes are pinned on fulfilling these dreams.

But why? Perhaps because we think we can determine our future. However, we tend to forget that every future has a past, and that our past is the foundation on which our future is built.

That's why the important question is not 'How do I imagine my future?' but 'How do I create a connection, a bridge, between the past (e.g. of a project) and the future?' This model, inspired by a visual planning system developed by The Grove consulting agency, helps you to work out what was relevant in your past and what you can forget, and what you should take with you from your past into the future.

This is how it works: you define a timeframe – e.g. the last year, your schooldays, your marriage, or from the founding of a company to today – and think back to the start of that period, either alone or in a group. Then add the following to the timeline:

- the people involved
- your goals (at the time)
- the successes
- the obstacles you overcame

- what you learned

The filled-in model reveals the importance you attach to your past.

Memory is the only paradise from which we cannot be driven.
Jean Paul

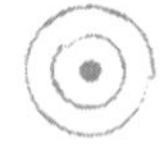

GOALS
(at the time)

WHAT YOU LEARNED

OBSTACLES
(that you overcame)

SUCCESSES

PEOPLE

Choose a timeframe and note the following: What were your goals? What did you learn? What obstacles did you overcome? What were your successes? Which people played an important role?

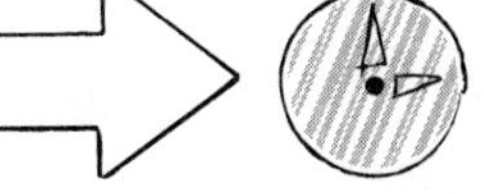

THE PERSONAL POTENTIAL TRAP

WHY IT IS BETTER NOT TO EXPECT ANYTHING

'Such a promising boy' – anybody who has heard this said about them can already guess what lies behind the personal potential trap: a lifetime of striving to fulfil this promise.

It is the curse of talented people. 'He just needs to find out what he really wants,' people say. His shortcomings are overlooked and his successes admired for the ease with which they are achieved. To begin with, he profits from this attractive yet fatal combination of talent and charisma. That is, until the stupid ones become hard-working: then he has to watch from the sidelines as he is overtaken by precisely those people who had once enviously looked up to him.

The personal potential trap can be precisely traced. In the model are three curves:

- my expectations of myself
- other people's expectations of me
- my actual achievements

The trap opens as soon as others' expectations of you and your actual achievements diverge too much. Normally a talented person cruises along until a crisis point is reached. The way to go is to promise 80 and deliver 120.

Are you prepared to expect less of yourself than what you think others expect of you?

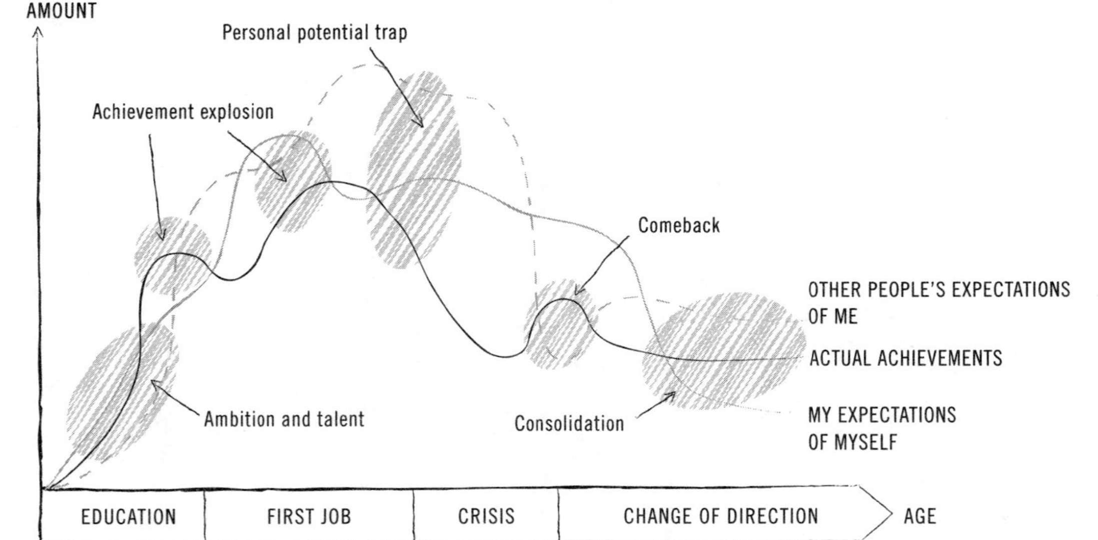

The model shows three curves: my own expectations, the expectations of others and my achievements. If the three diverge too much, you will fall into the personal potential trap.

THE HYPE CYCLE

HOW TO IDENTIFY THE NEXT BIG THING

Here are some questions that the smartest people in some of the biggest companies are pondering right now: Will Facebook survive? Will Microsoft's 'Bing' evolve? What will be the next big thing? Will it be relevant and useful – and will people love it?

Noboby knows the answers to these questions, but the people at Stamford consulting company Gartner might know more than most. They have invented a model called the 'hype cycle' to characterise the 'über-enthusiasm' or hype and subsequent disappointment that typically come with new technologies.

What people love about technology is, basically, that it works. Emailing works. The internet, if you have a bit of time on your hands, works. Text messaging works. What do they all have in common? They all went through each of the five phases of the hype cycle:

1. **Technology trigger**. The product is on the market and you hear about it everywhere: 'Have you checked this out?'

2. **Peak of inflated expectations**. The hype is at its peak. But people start to find mistakes. You hear: 'Yeah, it's great, but ...'

3. **Trough of disillusionment**. The product fails to meet expectations. The not-so-cool people use it. You hear: 'It's *so* four years ago.'

4. **Slope of enlightenment**. The media have stopped covering the technology, the hype is over. This is when many technologies simply fall out of the market. But some businesses might continue to experiment. They might change the original

version or find new uses for it. You hear: 'I never thought of it before, but you could use this in a different way ...'

5. **Plateau of productivity**. The benefits of the technology become widely demonstrated and accepted. Often it is the 2.0 or 3.0 version that emerges from the experimental phase to become a success. You hear ... nothing any more. People simply use it.

Love is for ever as long as it lasts.

➥See also: The chasm (p.114)

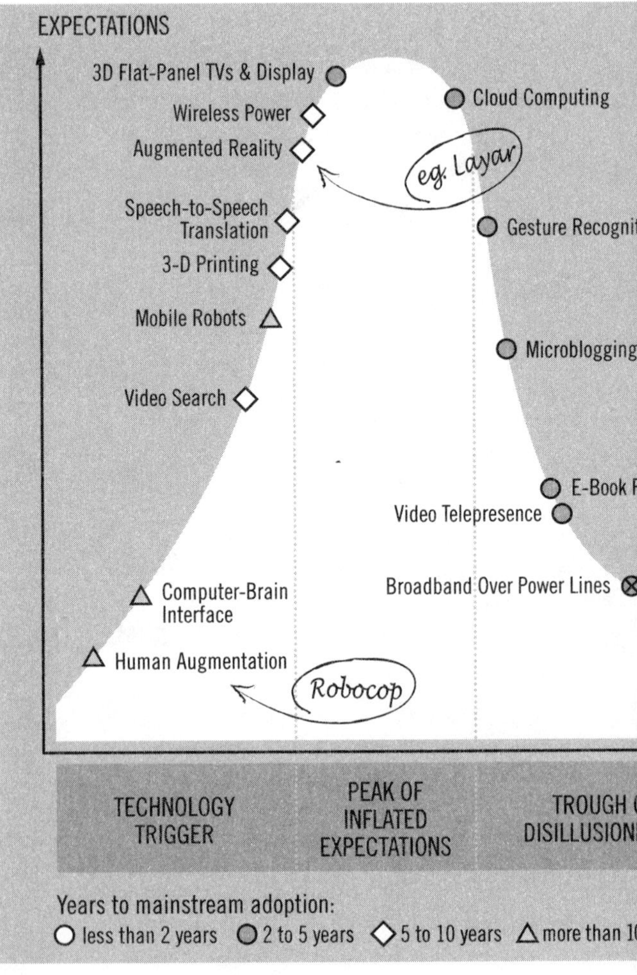

The hype cycle may also apply to relationships: in the beginning you're on top of the world. Then you start having second thoughts. After a certain time you either split up or make a long-term commitment.

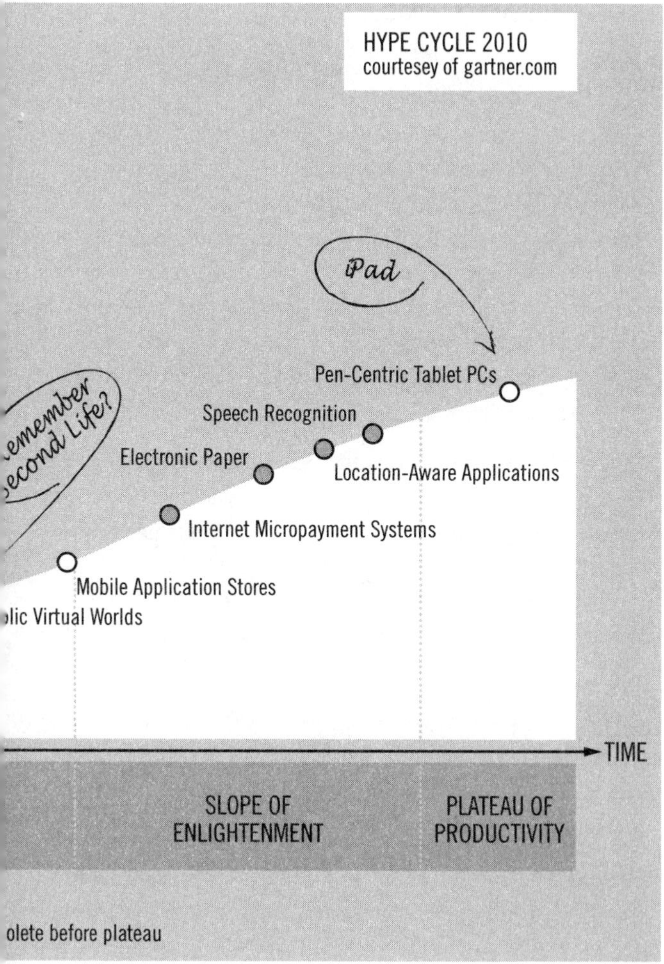

HYPE CYCLE 2010
courtesey of gartner.com

iPad

Pen-Centric Tablet PCs

emember
econd Life?

Speech Recognition

Electronic Paper

Location-Aware Applications

Internet Micropayment Systems

Mobile Application Stores

lic Virtual Worlds

TIME

SLOPE OF
ENLIGHTENMENT

PLATEAU OF
PRODUCTIVITY

olete before plateau

THE SUBTLE SIGNALS MODEL

WHY NUANCES MATTER

Anybody who works with people knows that information doesn't always flow to where it is meant to flow, that departments fight each other rather than support each other, and that managers base their decisions on cool-sounding strategies rather than on actual facts. In the words of the organisation theorist Elliott Jaques, 'Management is in the same state today that the natural sciences were in during the seventeenth century. There is not one single, well-established concept in the field of management on which you can build a testable theory.'

Why do some teams work well together and others badly? What are the subtle differences between functioning and non-functioning structures? The answer is that we don't know. But what we do know, thanks to US journalist Mark Buchanan, is that communication is vital for a healthy working environment, and that communication takes place on two levels: what we say, and how we say it.

MIT's Media Lab monitored creative teams at a major bank in order to find the answers to these questions: Who is saying what to whom? Who moves when, how often and where to? In what tone of voice is A speaking to B? Who is stressed, who seems to be suffering from burnout?

What sounds like Big Brother is called 'reality mining', and in the case of the bank it revealed the following: that those who talked a lot with others and who read a lot of emails – private as well as work-related – seemed to be generally happier and also more productive than those who concentrated only on work.

Who do you talk to most of all? Whose opinion do you value most?

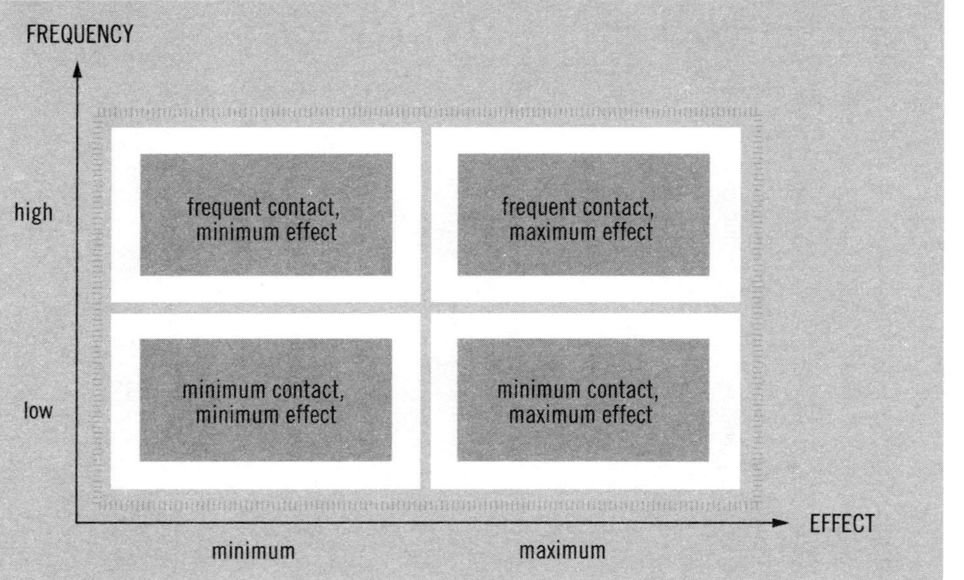

With whom do you speak and how often, and what are the consequences of your discussions? Arrange your discussions with colleagues in the matrix.

THE NETWORK TARGET MODEL

WHAT YOUR FRIENDS SAY ABOUT YOU

Could you say who your five best friends are? And could you say with which five people you communicate the most? And could you also say what all your acquaintanceships have in common?

The following model attempts to structure your contacts on the basis of your address book. Go through your contacts list and divide up your contacts according to the following criteria: who you see and how often, and to which group (friends, family, acquaintances, colleagues) they belong.

This is also interesting: go through your address book and note down

- how many are richer and how many are poorer than you
- how many are younger and how many are older than you
- how many do you think are more attractive than you, and how many are less attractive
- how many are the same nationality as you, and how many are of another nationality.

A man who doesn't spend time with his family can never be a real man. *Don Corleone*

➥See also: Family tree model (p.26)

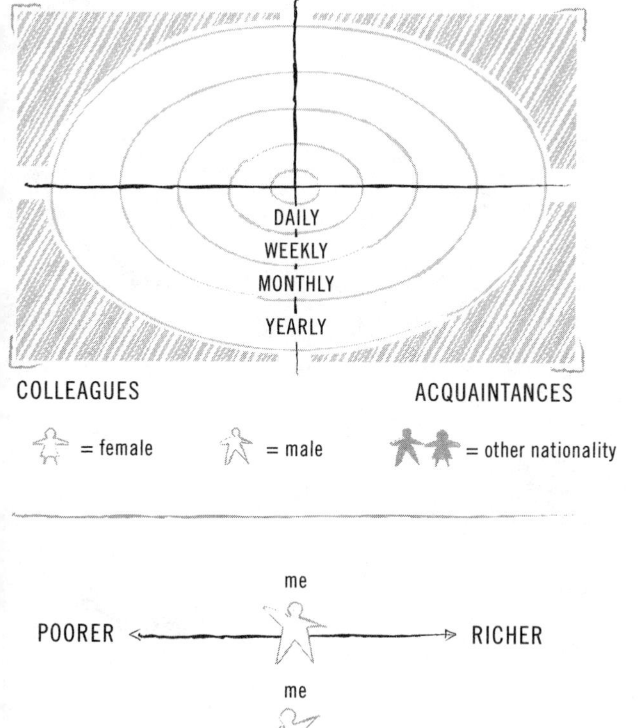

me

OLDER YOUNGER

me

UGLIER MORE ATTRACTIVE

In the model, insert the names of your friends and colleagues and how often you see them. Who would you like to see more of? Who would you prefer to see less of?

THE SUPERFICIAL KNOWLEDGE MODEL

EVERYTHING YOU DON'T NEED TO KNOW

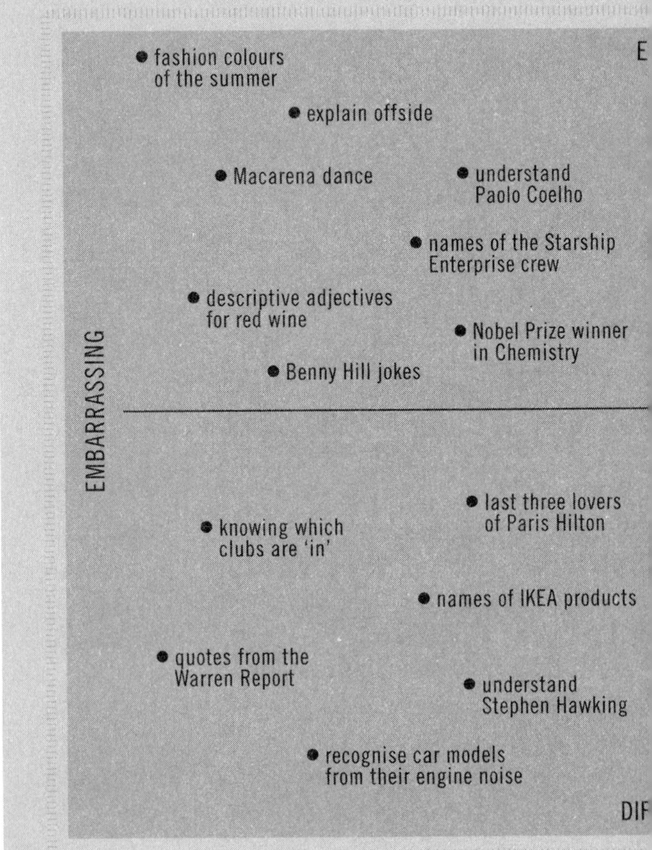

Knowledge can impress people – or bore them. What do you know? Begin with the top right field.

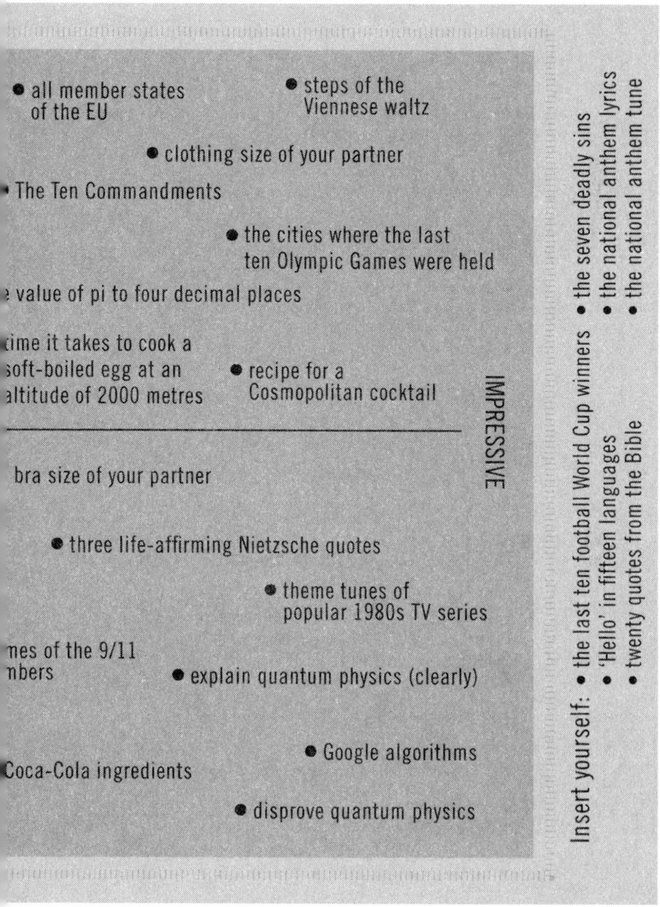

- all member states of the EU
- steps of the Viennese waltz
- clothing size of your partner
- The Ten Commandments
- the cities where the last ten Olympic Games were held
- value of pi to four decimal places
- time it takes to cook a soft-boiled egg at an altitude of 2000 metres
- recipe for a Cosmopolitan cocktail

IMPRESSIVE

- bra size of your partner
- three life-affirming Nietzsche quotes
- theme tunes of popular 1980s TV series
- mes of the 9/11 mbers
- explain quantum physics (clearly)
- Google algorithms
- Coca-Cola ingredients
- disprove quantum physics

Insert yourself: • the last ten football World Cup winners • the seven deadly sins
• 'Hello' in fifteen languages • the national anthem lyrics
• twenty quotes from the Bible • the national anthem tune

HOW TO UNDERSTAND OTHERS BETTER

THE SWISS CHEESE MODEL

HOW MISTAKES HAPPEN

Everyone makes mistakes. Some people learn from them, while others repeat them. Here is what you need to know about mistakes.

There are different types of mistake:

- real mistakes – occur when the wrong process is carried out
- black-outs – occur when part of a process is forgotten
- slip-ups – occur when the right process is carried out incorrectly

There are various levels on which mistakes occur:

- skill-based level
- rule-based level
- knowledge-based level

And there are various factors that contribute to mistakes occurring:

- people involved– boss, team, colleagues, friends
- technical provisions – equipment, workplace
- organisational elements – task to be fulfilled, timing
- outside influences – time, economic climate, mood, weather

The most impressive illustration of the causes and effects of mistakes is the human error or Swiss cheese model by James Reason (1990). The model compares the different levels on which mistakes occur with slices of Emmental cheese. In a mistake-free world, the cheese would have no holes. But in the real world, the cheese is cut into thin slices, and every slice has many holes that are in different places in different slices. Imagine the holes as conduits for mistakes. A mistake remains unnoticed or irrelevant if it penetrates only one hole in one of the slices. But it can lead to catastrophe if the holes in the different slices align and the mistake passes through all the holes in all of the defences. The model can be used in the fields of medicine and air traffic, for example – and anywhere where mistakes can have fatal consequences.

Experience is the name everyone gives to his mistakes. *Oscar Wilde*

➥See also: Results optimisation model (p.146)

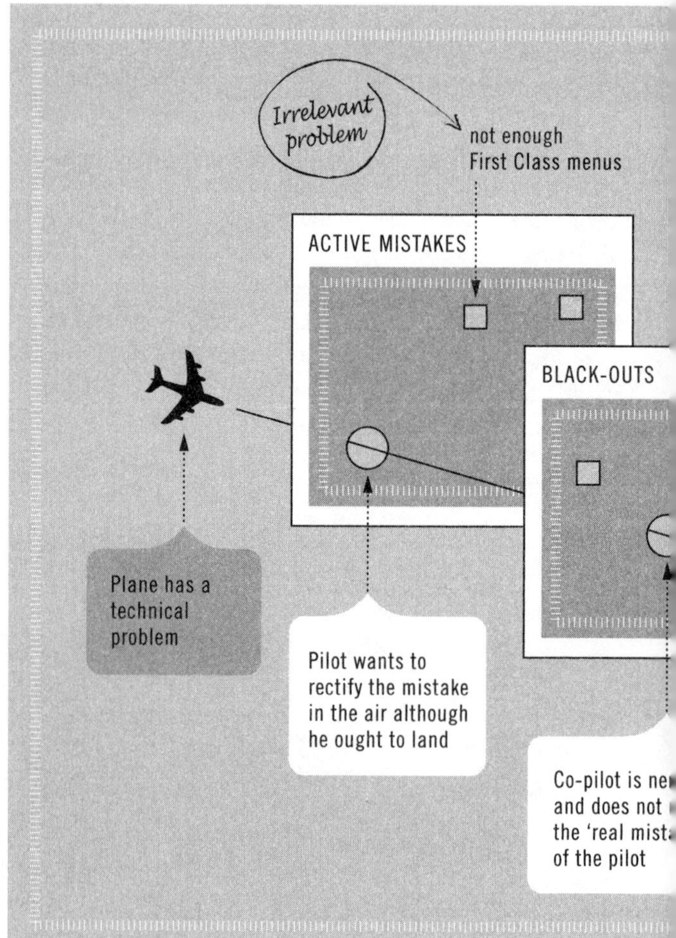

The illustration shows what happens when mistakes are made on three different levels, and three 'holes in the cheese' align: 1. The pilot makes a mistake. 2. The co-pilot reacts incorrectly. 3. While attempting to rectify the mistake, another is made.

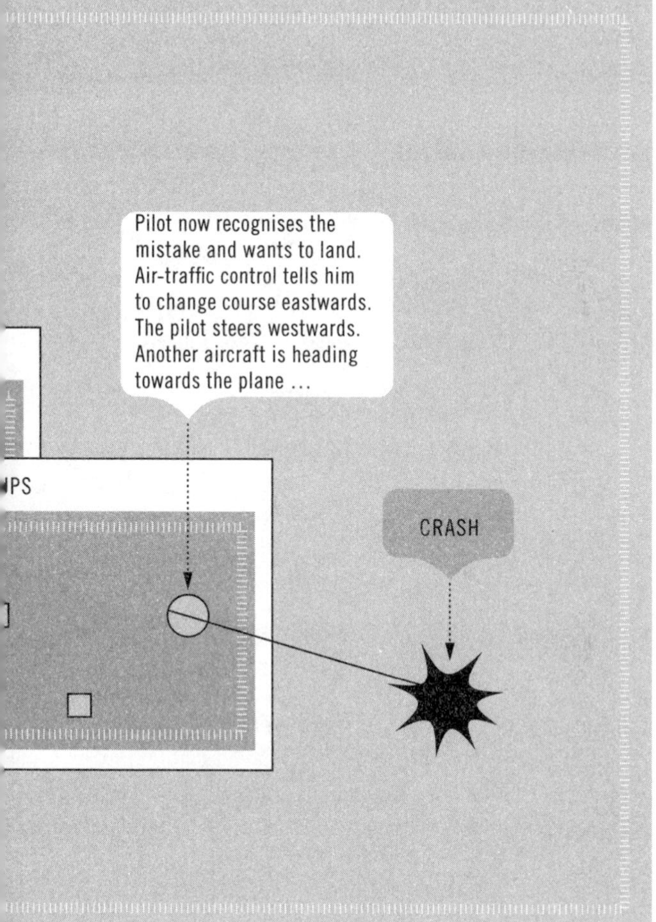
Pilot now recognises the mistake and wants to land. Air-traffic control tells him to change course eastwards. The pilot steers westwards. Another aircraft is heading towards the plane ...
PS
CRASH

THE MASLOW PYRAMIDS

WHAT YOU ACTUALLY NEED, WHAT YOU ACTUALLY WANT

'The three most important questions,' begins the 2003 German film *Hierankl*, 'are: Are you having sex? Do you have a family? Are you intellectually stimulated? Scoring three yeses is paradise; two yeses is what you need to be happy, and one yes is what you need to survive.' The film is bad, but the questions it asks are good.

In 1943, the psychologist Abraham Maslow published a 'hierarchy of needs' model. He categorised human needs as follows:

- physiological needs (eating, sleeping, warmth, sex)
- security (somewhere to live, job security, health, protection against adversities)
- social relationships (friends, partner, love)
- recognition (status, power, money)
- self-actualisation (individuality, realising personal potential, but also faith and transcendence)

The first three of these are basic needs. If they are satisfied, a person no longer thinks about them. The last two are aspirations or personal growth needs; they can never really be satisfied. The pyramids model becomes interesting if we contrast our aspirations with our needs.

Rule of thumb for the Western world: the things we desire the most are the things we need the least.

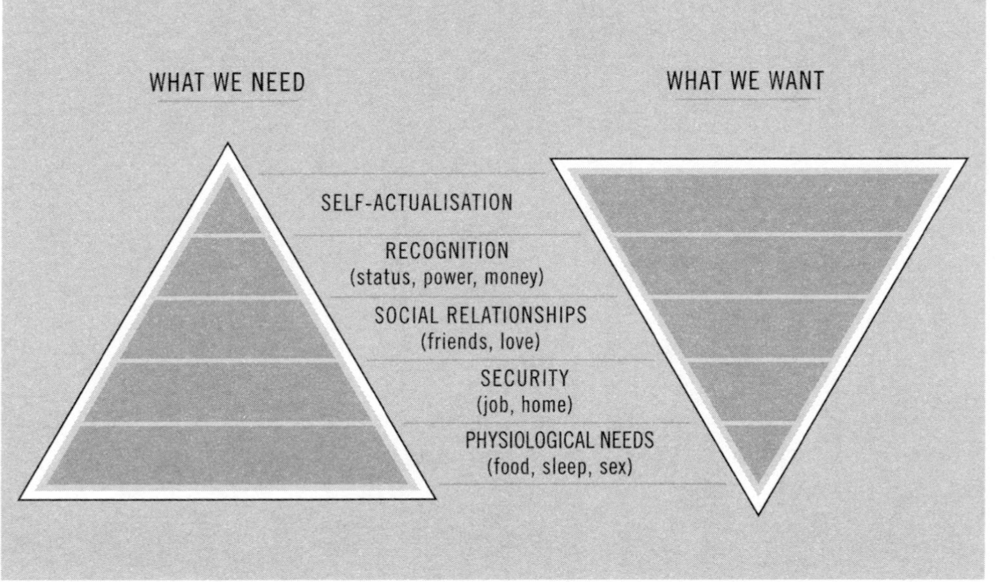

Create your own personal basic needs pyramids: What do you have? What do you want?

THINKING OUTSIDE THE BOX

HOW TO COME UP WITH BRILLIANT IDEAS

A really innovative idea – rather than an old idea that has been applied to a new context, or a variation of an existing idea – is rare. Innovative ideas usually emerge when we leave our comfort zone, or when we break the rules. The example used here is the 'nine-point problem', which first appeared in puzzle magazines at the beginning of the twentieth century.

The task: Connect the nine points using a maximum of four straight lines without lifting your pen from the paper.

The solution: The trick is to extend the lines outside the box.

This puzzle is often used as an example of creative thinking. But don't jump to any rash conclusions – because Dr Peter Suedfeld, a professor of psychology at the University of British Columbia, made an interesting observation. He developed the Restricted Environmental Stimulation Technique (REST), which involves a person spending time in a darkened room with no visual or auditory stimulation. Suedfeld noticed that the subjects of the experiment didn't go mad. On the contrary: their blood pressure went down, their mood improved and they became more creative.

A person who wants to think outside the box is better off thinking inside a box.

➥See also: Morphological box and SCAMPER (p.28)

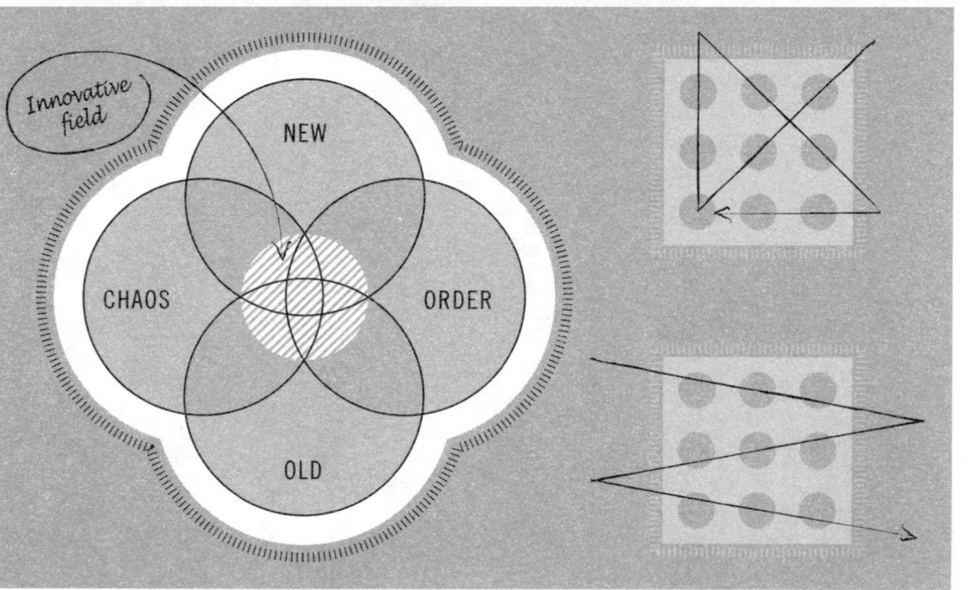

Left: 'outside the box' is the area where the known and unknown overlap. Right: two ways to connect the nine points with four lines.

THE SINUS MILIEU AND BOURDIEU MODELS

WHERE YOU BELONG

The Sinus Milieu is a psychographic method for establishing the different socio-cultural groupings to which a person belongs. It is often used in marketing to define target groups. The idea was developed by the French sociologist Emile Durkheim. On the next double page is a rarely used version by another French sociologist, Pierre Bourdieu, in the form of an axis model. Bourdieu's analysis of cultural consumption challenges us to think about our deep-rooted cultural preferences and practices.

The narrowness of the Sinus groups is often criticised. It is true that it cannot answer the question 'Where do I belong if my father was a bus-driver, my mother a hippy, I am a fashion designer and in my spare time I hang out with my friends from the golf club?' The popularity of the model can be explained by the lock-in principle: if we get used to something, we don't want to change our habits, even if we are presented with something new or different that might be better.

Nearly all market research and market analyses use the Sinus Milieu model, despite its limitations. It shows us that if a majority have become used to one system, it is difficult for another system to establish itself. Habit is stronger than the desire for improvement.

Our origins are our future. *Martin Heidegger*

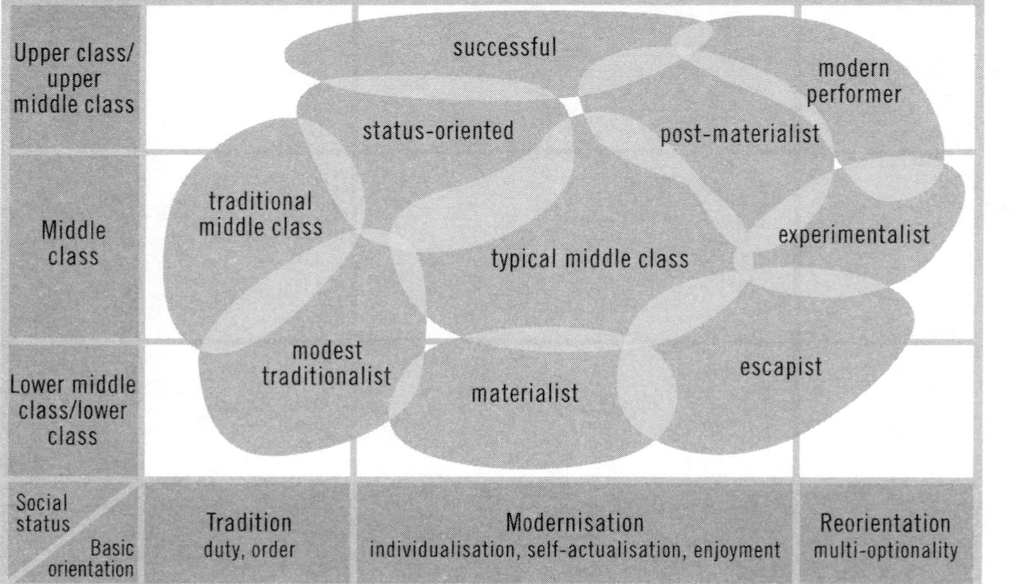

Where would you position yourself? Where would you position your parents? Where would you like to be positioned?

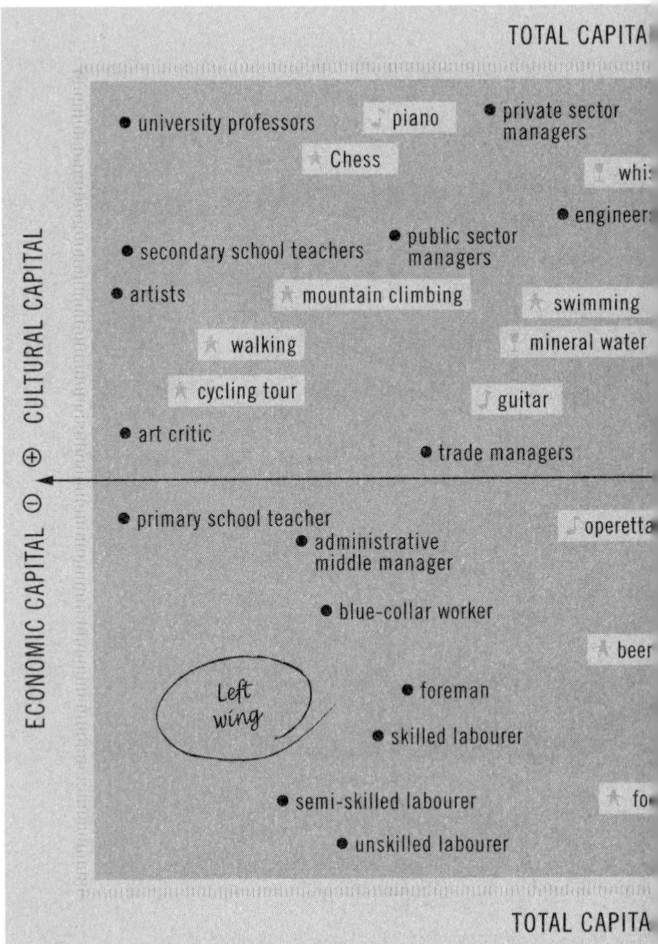

Bourdieu model: Where would you position yourself? Where would you position your parents? And where would you like to be positioned?

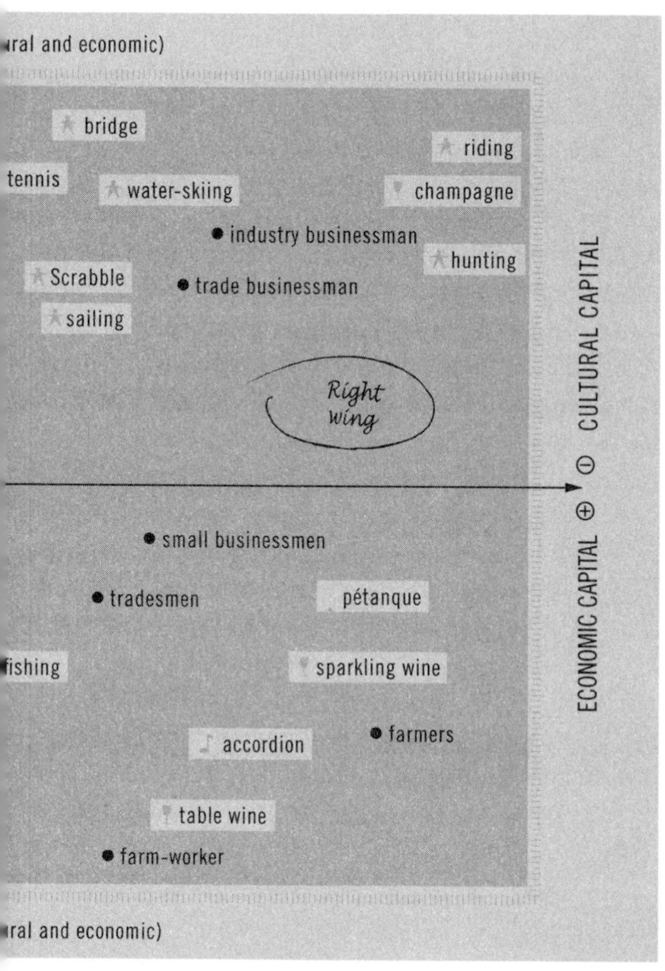
ral and economic)
bridge
riding
tennis
water-skiing
champagne
industry businessman
hunting
Scrabble
trade businessman
sailing
Right wing
CULTURAL CAPITAL ⊖
ECONOMIC CAPITAL ⊕
small businessmen
tradesmen
pétanque
fishing
sparkling wine
accordion
farmers
table wine
farm-worker
ral and economic)

THE DOUBLE-LOOP LEARNING MODEL

HOW TO LEARN FROM YOUR MISTAKES

Double-loop learning involves reflecting on your actions and learning from them. The theory is based on the work of the system theoreticians Heinz von Foerster and Niklas Luhmann, in particular on the idea of 'second-order observation'. Strictly speaking, this is not a model but a technique for know-alls. How can you master this desirable technique? Simple: you learn how to observe first-order observers.

First-order observers see things as they appear to them. For them, the world is simply there. Second-order observers, on the other hand, attribute *what* the first-order observers see to *how* they see it. In other words, second-order observers observe a way of observing. If, for example, you criticise a football referee for making a wrong decision, you are a second-order observer: your perspective is different from the referee's because you are one step removed from the game and not actually calling the play, and you think that makes you a better judge.

During the act of observing, first-order observers are unaware of their own way of observing – it is their blind spot. Recognising this blind spot enables second-order observers to become know-alls. They are able to point out to the first-order observers that it is possible to observe differently and thus see things differently.

The psychologist Chris Argyris and the philosopher Donald Schön developed double-loop learning out of these theoretical ideas on observation. In the best-case scenario, the single loop (the first-order observation) is best practice. Something that works well is not changed but simply repeated. In the worst-case scenario it is worst practice – the same mistake is repeated, or a problem is solved without questioning how it arose in the first place.

In double-loop learning you think about and question what you are doing, and try to break your own pattern, not simply by doing something differently, but by thinking about why you do it the way you do it. What are the objectives and values behind your actions? If you are fully aware of these, you may be able to change them.

The problem inherent in the double loop is the discrepancy between what we say we are about to do (known as espoused theory) and what we actually do (known as theory in use). If we really want to change something, it is not enough to create guidelines for our employees or ourselves, or to give directives. These only reach us as a command (espoused theory). Real changes occur when we reassess our more deeply rooted reasons, objectives and values. These are the 'force fields' that affect the theory in use.

Be the change you want to see.

➥See also: Black box model (p.118), The world's next top model (p.148)

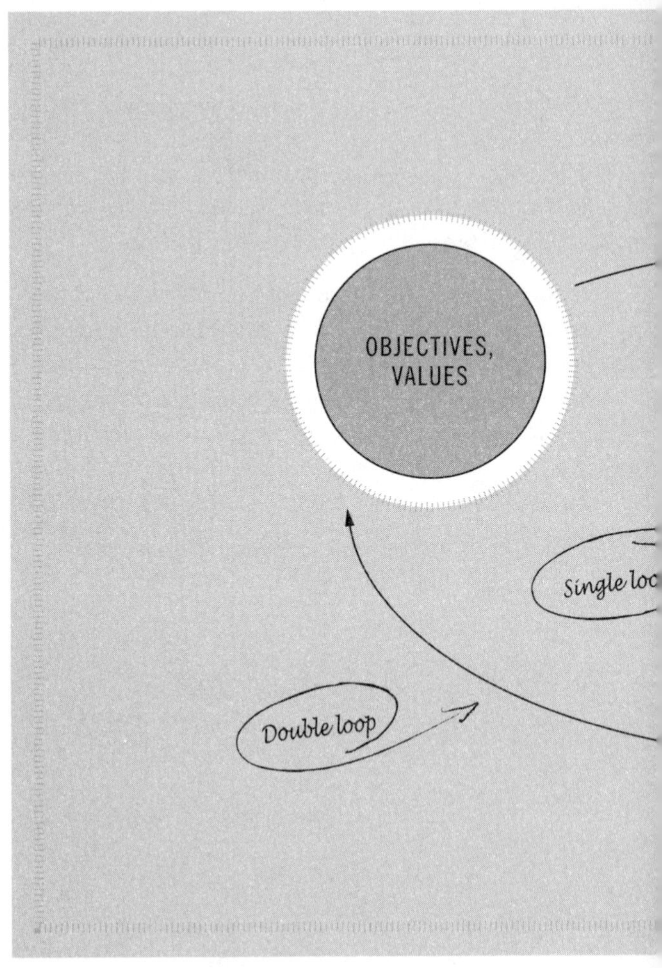

When was the last time you broke a familiar pattern in your life and really did something differently? Which pattern would you like to break? What is preventing you from breaking it?

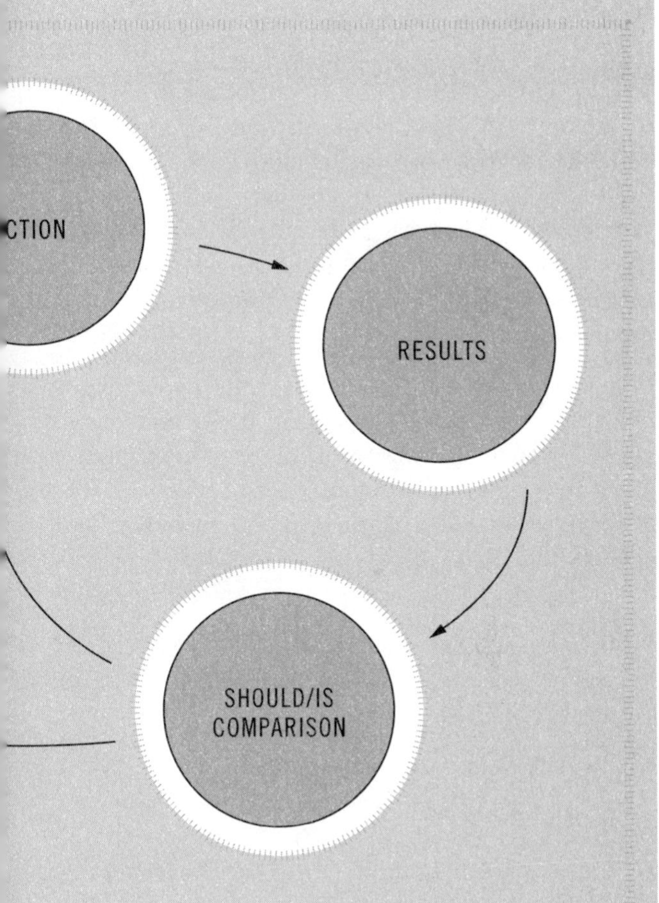
CTION
RESULTS
SHOULD/IS
COMPARISON

THE AI MODEL

WHAT KIND OF DISCUSSION TYPE ARE YOU?

The abbreviation AI stands for Appreciative Inquiry, a method attributed to the American management expert David Cooperrider that involves concentrating on the strengths, positive attributes and potential of a company or a person, rather than weaknesses. 'What is going really well at the moment?' replaces the classic question 'What is the problem?' Concentrating on weakness creates a negative impression from the outset.

Every person, every system, every product, every idea has faults. In the best-case scenario, an awareness of this fact can lead to a determined pursuit of perfection. But in many cases, focusing too strongly on the flaws of an idea or project stifles the open and positive approach that is essential for good working practices. The basic principle is to take an idea that is not yet fully developed and to continue developing it, instead of prematurely abandoning it.

People often reveal their character in their approach to discussions. Four basic types can be identified, according to how people react to suggestions:

- **The fault-finder**: 'The idea is good, but ...'
- **The dictator**: 'No!'
- **The schoolteacher**: 'No, the idea isn't good because ...'
- **The AI thinker**: 'Yes, and we could also ...'

Any fool can criticise. And most fools do. *Benjamin Franklin*

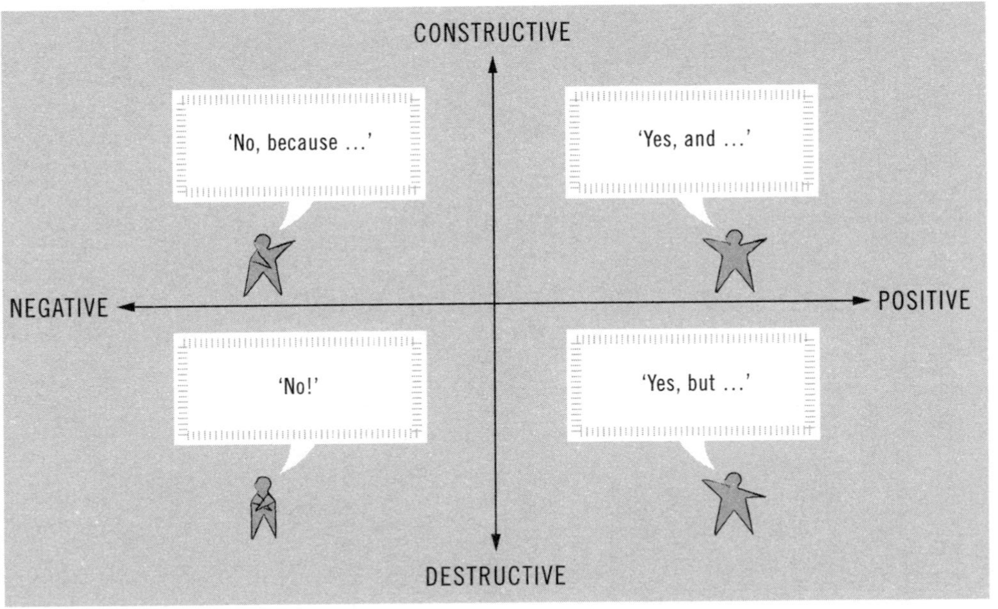

The next time you are in a group discussion, make a note of how each person presents their arguments.

THE SMALL-WORLD MODEL

HOW SMALL THE WORLD REALLY IS

In 1967, the social psychologist Stanley Milgram claimed that every person in the world is connected to every other person by just a few degrees of separation – a maximum of six, to be precise. In the 1990s, the model experienced a renaissance as a party game: 'I know somebody who knows somebody else who knows somebody else ...'

In this way you can connect yourself to practically any famous person in the world – or you can connect all actors that have ever appeared in a film to one another. Surprisingly, Laurence Olivier is only two steps away from Pamela Anderson. Pamela Anderson appeared in *Snap Dragon* (1993) with James Wing Woo, who in turn appeared in *Marathon Man* (1976) with Laurence Olivier. If you don't believe it, check out the website oracleofbacon.org.

The small-world phenomenon becomes even more interesting when it comes to viral marketing: who do you know who could spread the word about your idea or product? Social networks like LinkedIn and Facebook show how many contacts you have and through how many other people you know these contacts.

It's not about what you can do, but about who you know.

➥See also: Family tree model (p.26), Subtle signals model (p.78)

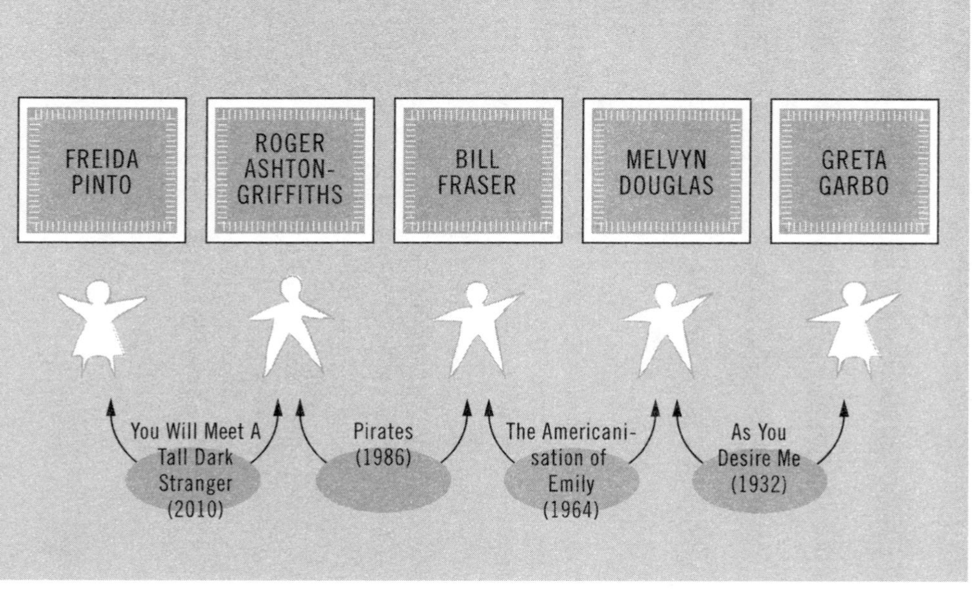

How many degrees of separation do you think there are between you and Greta Garbo?

THE PARETO PRINCIPLE

WHY 80 PER CENT OF THE OUTPUT IS ACHIEVED WITH 20 PER CENT OF THE INPUT

At the beginning of the twentieth century, the Italian economist Vilfredo Pareto observed that 80 per cent of Italy's wealth belonged to 20 per cent of the population. And that's not all: 20 per cent of workers do 80 per cent of the work; 20 per cent of criminals commit 80 per cent of the crimes; 20 per cent of car drivers cause 80 per cent of the accidents; 20 percent of hedge funds invest 80 per cent of the money; 20 per cent of pub-goers consume 80 per cent of the alcohol. We wear 20 per cent of the clothes we have in our wardrobes and spend 80 per cent of our time with 20 per cent of our friends. In business meetings, 80 per cent of the decisions are made in 20 per cent of the time, and 20 per cent of a company's clients (products) are responsible for 80 per cent of its turnover.

Of course, the Pareto rule cannot be applied to everything (mathematicians prefer the more precise '64/4' rule, because 80 per cent of 80 is 64 and 20 per cent of 20 is 4). But anybody who wants to plan their time optimally should know that roughly 20 per cent of the time spent on a task leads to 80 per cent of the results.

I am definitely going to take a course on time management ... just as soon as I can work it into my schedule. *Louis E. Boone*

➥See also: Long-tail model (p.108)

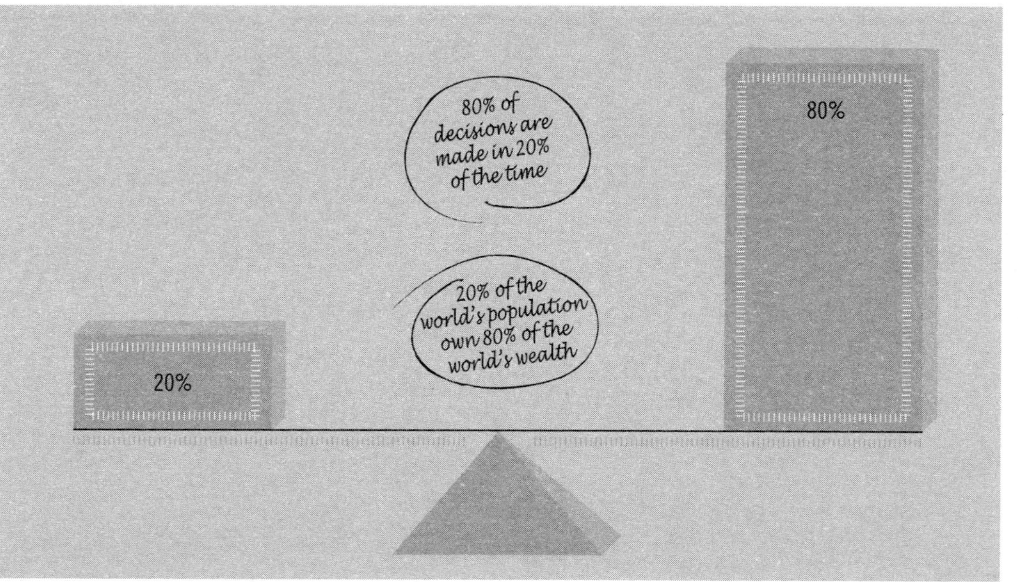
80% of decisions are made in 20% of the time
20% of the world's population own 80% of the world's wealth
20%
80%

The Pareto principle describes the statistical phenomenon whereby a small number of high values contribute more to the total than a high number of low values.

THE LONG-TAIL MODEL

HOW THE INTERNET IS TRANSFORMING THE ECONOMY

The 'Pareto Principle' – the idea that 20 per cent of products generate 80 per cent of turnover – may not always be right. In 2004, the editor-in-chief of *Wired*, Chris Anderson, claimed that nearly everything that is offered for sale on the internet is also actually sold – however bizarre or unnecessary the product. It appears that business is gravitating to where there is variety instead of uniformity.

Anderson used a demand curve to illustrate his claim. On the far left, the curve rises sharply upwards. Here are the best-sellers and blockbusters that account for 20 per cent of the market. Then the curve levels out gently to the right. This is where we find the less popular books and films. This part of the curve is much wider, spanning many more products, than the peak. Instinctively one would think the Pareto principle is right: the best-sellers (20 per cent) are more profitable than the 'rest-sellers' (80 per cent). But the figures suggest something different: the long tail (as Anderson calls it), achieves a higher turnover than the few best-sellers.

The internet is the world's largest library. It's just that all the books are on the floor. *John Allen Paulos*

➥See also: Pareto principle (p.106)

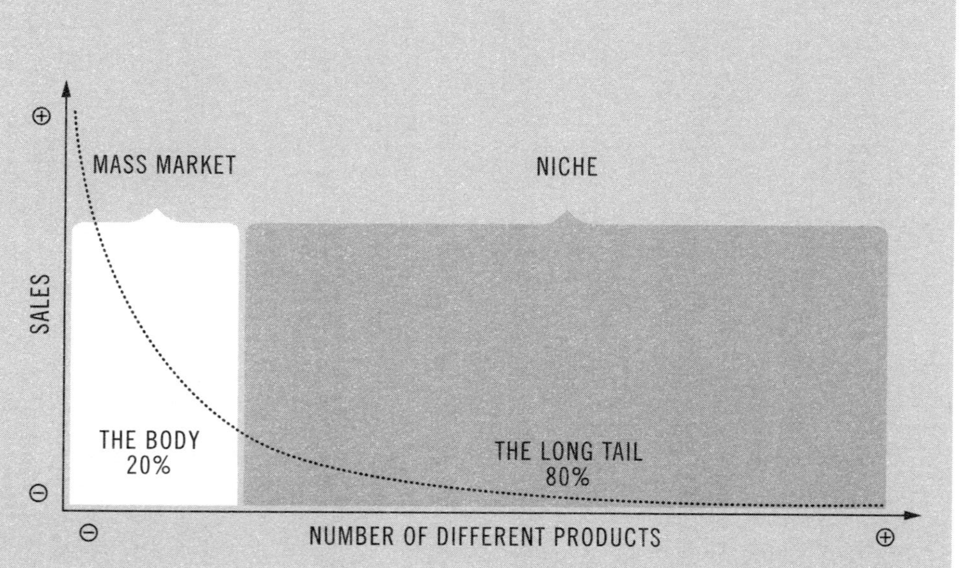

The mass market wants best-sellers, but there is also a demand for niche products. Individual demand may be low, but collectively the niche products are worth more than the best-sellers.

THE MONTE CARLO SIMULATION

WHY WE CAN ONLY APPROXIMATE A DEFINITIVE OUTCOME

The number pi (3.1415927...) is what mathematicians call irrational. It can never be written out in full: it continues for an infinite number of decimal places, in a seemingly random sequence of digits. Randomness is found in many phenomena that we would like to be able to predict, such as changes in the weather or the movements of share prices. Inspired by the casino city of Monte Carlo, a computer simulation method has been developed to calculate these apparently incalculable phenomena.

If you roll a dice, you know that you will roll a 1, 2, 3, 4, 5 or 6. But you don't know which of these numbers you will get with a given roll. This is exactly how the Monte Carlo simulation works: by running multiple trials based on random sampling to determine an outcome, using a combination of probability calculation and statistics.

Why is the Monte Carlo model important? Because it reminds us that models do not represent reality, but are simply an approximation of reality.

If I know exactly what I'm going to do, what's the good in doing it?
Pablo Picasso

➡See also: Black box model (p.118), Black swan model (p.112), The world's next top model (p.148)

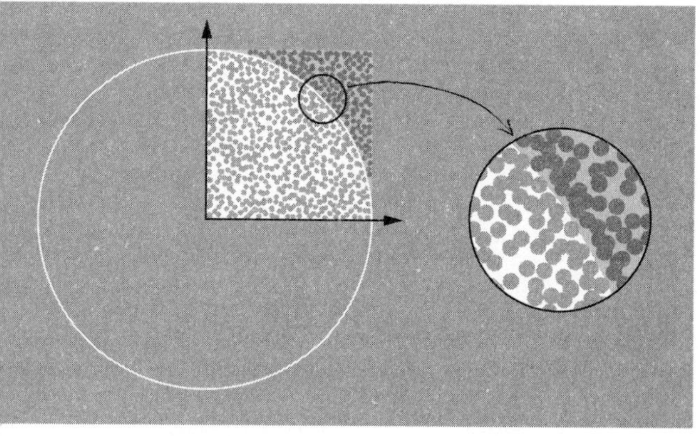

In this example, you want to predict where a dot is likely to land. To do so, you let hundreds of dots 'rain' randomly onto the square, and count how many land inside and how many outside the quarter-circle. You repeat the process many times. Your result is determined statistically (if the majority of the dots usually land inside the circle, you can predict that this is where your dot is likely to land in future), but there is still a certain margin of error.

THE BLACK SWAN MODEL

WHY YOUR EXPERIENCES DON'T MAKE YOU ANY WISER

Here are three questions for a reflective person: How do we know what we know? Does the past help us predict the future? Why do we never expect unexpected events?

In his 1912 book *The Problems of Philosophy*, Bertrand Russell summarised the answers to all three questions: a chicken that expects to be fed every day assumes that it will continue to be fed every day. It starts to firmly believe that humans are kind. Nothing in the chicken's life points to the fact that one day it will be slaughtered.

We humans also have to acknowledge that the biggest catastrophes usually come as a complete surprise to us. That's why, according to Russell, we should always question the things we take for granted.

For example, when two Boeing airliners were flown into the World Trade Center, the public was shocked – the catastrophe seemed to strike completely without warning. However, in the weeks and months following 11 September 2001, it seemed that practically everything had pointed towards this attack.

The Lebanese writer Nassim Nicholas Taleb calls this phenomenon – our inability to predict the future from the past – the black swan. In the Western world it was always assumed that all swans were white – until naturalists in the seventeenth century discovered a breed of black swans. What had hitherto been unimaginable was suddenly taken for granted.

Taleb's black swan thesis is not really a model, but a re.jection of the cause-and-effect principle. And it reminds us that we tend to cling most tightly to pillars that we see toppling.

What were the black swans – the unexpected events – in your life, and when did they occur?

➥See also: Black box model (p.118), The world's next top model (p.148)

THE CHASM – THE DIFFUSION MODEL

WHY EVERYBODY HAS AN IPOD

Why is it that some ideas – including stupid ones – take hold and become trends, while others bloom briefly before withering and disappearing from the public eye?

Sociologists describe the way in which a catchy idea or product becomes popular as 'diffusion'. One of the most famous diffusion studies is an analysis by Bruce Ryan and Neal Gross of the diffusion of hybrid corn in the 1930s in Greene County, Iowa. The new type of corn was better than the old sort in every way, yet it took twenty-two years for it to become widely accepted.

The diffusion researchers called the farmers who switched to the new corn as early as 1928 'innovators', and the somewhat bigger group that was infected by them 'early adaptors'. They were the opinion leaders in the communities, respected people who observed the experiments of the innovators and then joined them. They were followed at the end of the 1930s by the 'sceptical masses', those who would never change anything before it had been tried out by the successful farmers. But at some point even they were infected by the 'hybrid corn virus', and eventually transmitted it to the die-hard conservatives, the 'stragglers'.

Translated into a graph, this development takes the form of a curve typical of the progress of an epidemic. It rises, gradually at first, then reaches the critical point of any newly launched product, when many products fail. The critical point for any innovation is the transition from the early adaptors to the sceptics, for at this point there is a 'chasm'. According to the US sociologist Morton Grodzins, if the early adaptors succeed in getting the innovation across the chasm to the sceptical masses, the epidemic cycle reaches the tipping point. From there, the curve rises sharply when the masses accept the product, and sinks again when only the stragglers remain.

With technological innovations like the iPod or the iPhone, the cycle described above is very short. Interestingly, the early adaptors turn away from the product as soon as the critical masses have accepted it, in search of the next new thing. The chasm model was introduced by the American consultant and author Geoffrey Moore.

First they ignore you, then they laugh at you, then they fight you, then you win. *Mahatma Gandhi*

➥See also: Long-tail model (p.108), Pareto principle (p.102)

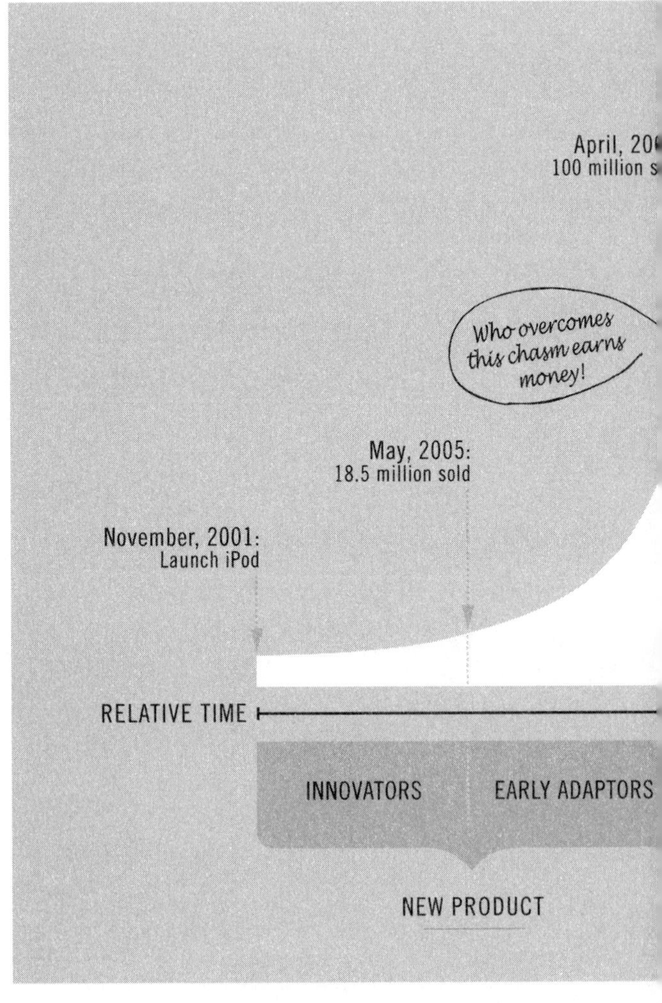

The model shows the typical curve of a product launch, taking the iPod as an example. At what point on the curve have you purchased an iPod?

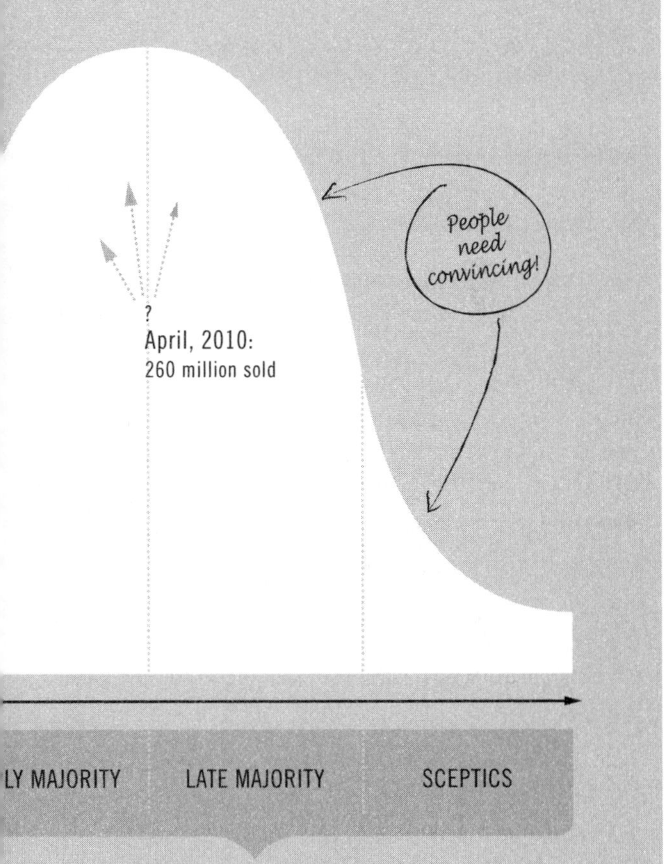

ESTABLISHED PRODUCT

THE BLACK BOX MODEL

WHY FAITH IS REPLACING KNOWLEDGE

One thing is undisputed: our world is getting more complicated all the time. Black and white, good and bad, right and wrong have been displaced by complicated constructs that leave most people in the dark.

As the world around us becomes increasingly fast-paced and complex, the amount that we really know – that we can really grasp and understand – decreases all the time. As recently as the 1980s, teachers still tried to explain to their pupils how computers worked, in terms of binary code. Today it is more or less taken for granted that we do not understand many of the things that surround us, such as mobile phones and iPods. And even if somebody tried to explain the DNA code to us, we would probably be out of our depth.

We are increasingly surrounded by 'black boxes', complex constructs that we do not understand even if they are explained to us. We cannot comprehend the inner processes of a black box, but none the less we integrate their inputs and outputs into our decision-making.

The amount that we simply *have* to believe, without understanding it, is increasing all the time. As a result, we are tending to assign more importance to those who can explain something than to their actual explanation.

In the future it will be the norm to convince people with images and emotions rather than with arguments.

➥See also: Black swan model (p.112)

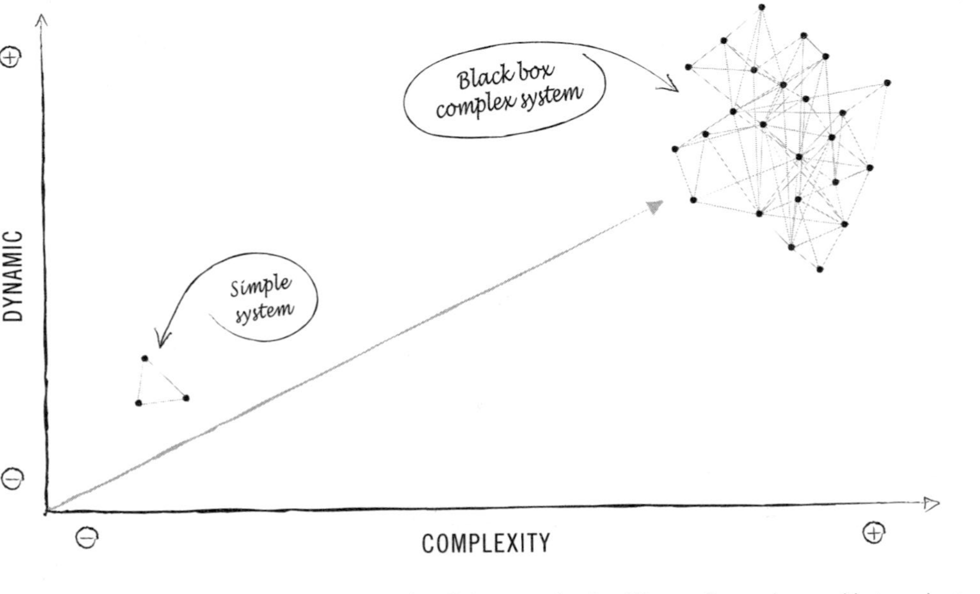

The speed and complexity of a process increase in relation to each other. We are often no longer able to understand increasingly complex explanations.

THE STATUS MODEL

HOW TO RECOGNISE A WINNER

Whether you wished you had been born into privilege, or were just a little richer, we all have social aspirations. But how can we recognise class distinctions and social status?

The model over the page has two axes: 'how you spend it' and 'how you earned it'. In the matrix we define four types:

OLD MONEY

The established elite can be characterised by their dogged adherence to old-school conventions in the face of a changing world. They drive two identical Rolls-Royces for fear of otherwise appearing too showy. They donate millions to charity to soothe their consciences. There is a touch of the ridiculous about them.

CHILDREN OF RICH PARENTS

Sound like a broken record searching for an identity that never was. Good for nothing. They should be routinely ignored.

THE NOUVEAU RICHE

Spend their money like there's no tomorrow – as conspicuously as possible so that everyone notices. The status symbol of this group is the monster SUV. However, their propensity for hysteria suggests that it could all be over soon.

THE GREEN SUVers

The creative career, organic lifestyle and green SUV, proclaim an alternative globalisation in which good conquers evil. But this sustainable way of life is motivated less by a bad conscience than by personal advantage. The green SUVers do not forgo luxury, because nowadays luxury is green. The metaphor of this new elite is the green SUV: sustainable luxury.

The poor wish to be rich, the rich wish to be happy, the single wish to be married, and the married wish to be dead. *Ann Landers*

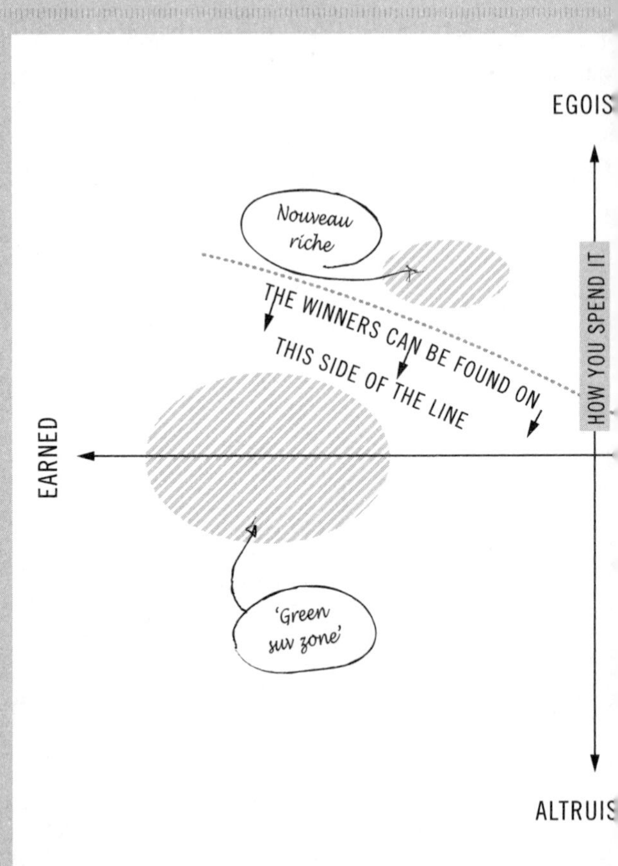
Nouveau riche
THE WINNERS CAN BE FOUND ON THIS SIDE OF THE LINE
HOW YOU SPEND IT
EARNED
'Green suv zone'

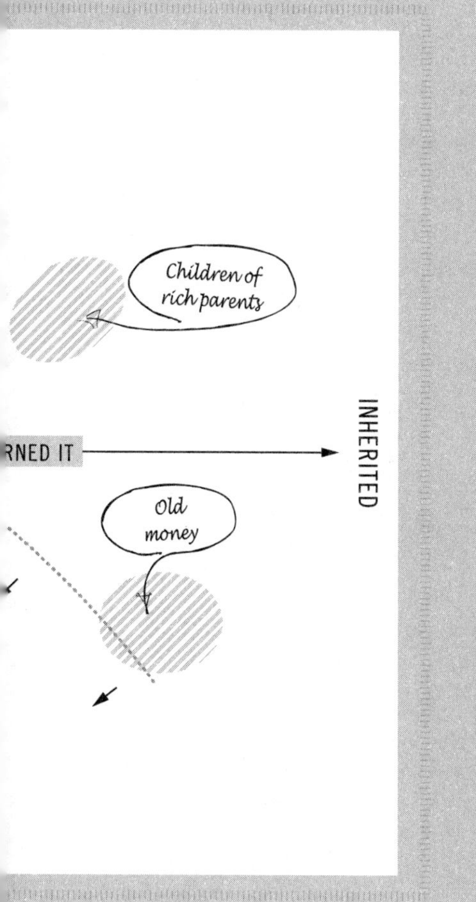
Children of rich parents
RNED IT
INHERITED
Old money

THE PRISONER'S DILEMMA

WHEN IS IT WORTH TRUSTING SOMEONE?

As the saying goes, 'Trust makes way for treachery'. But is this true? Here's a puzzle that provides an answer.

Two prisoners are suspected of having carried out a crime together. The maximum sentence for the crime is ten years. The two suspects have been arrested separately, and each is offered the same deal: if he confesses that they both committed the crime and his accomplice remains silent, the charges against him will be dropped – but his accomplice will have to serve the full ten years. If both he and his accomplice remain silent, there will only be circumstantial evidence, which will none the less be enough to put both men behind bars for two years. But if both he and his accomplice confess to the crime, they will both be sentenced to five years in prison. The suspects cannot confer. How should they react under questioning? Should they trust each other?

This is the so-called prisoner's dilemma, a classic conundrum in game theory. The two suspects both lose if they opt for the most obvious solution – i.e. to put themselves first: they get a five-year sentence each. They fare better if each one trusts that the other will remain silent: they then get a two-year sentence each. Note that if only one of the suspects confesses, then the sentence is ten years for the other suspect and the confessor is freed.

In 1979 the political scientist Robert Axelrod organised a tournament in which fourteen academic colleagues played 200 rounds of the prisoner's dilemma against one another in order to work out the best strategy. He found that in the first round it is best to cooperate with your accomplice (i.e. trust him). In the second round, do what your accomplice did in the previous round. By imitating his moves, he will follow yours.

You can't shake hands with a clenched fist. *Indira Gandhi*

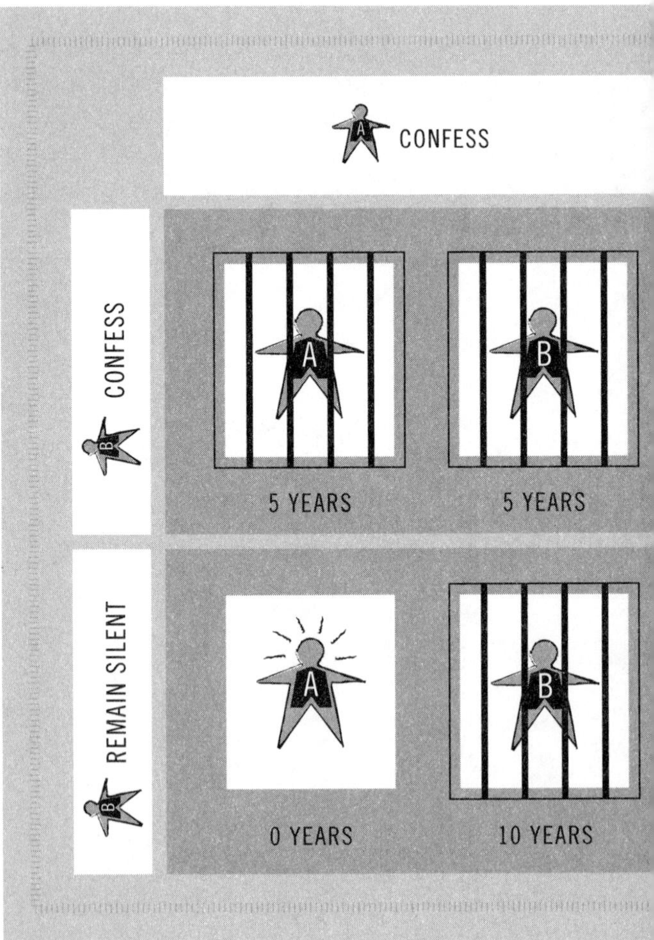

You and your accomplice are on trial. If only you confess, your accomplice will serve ten years. If you both remain silent, you will both serve two years. If both of you confess, you will both serve five years. You cannot confer. How should you react?

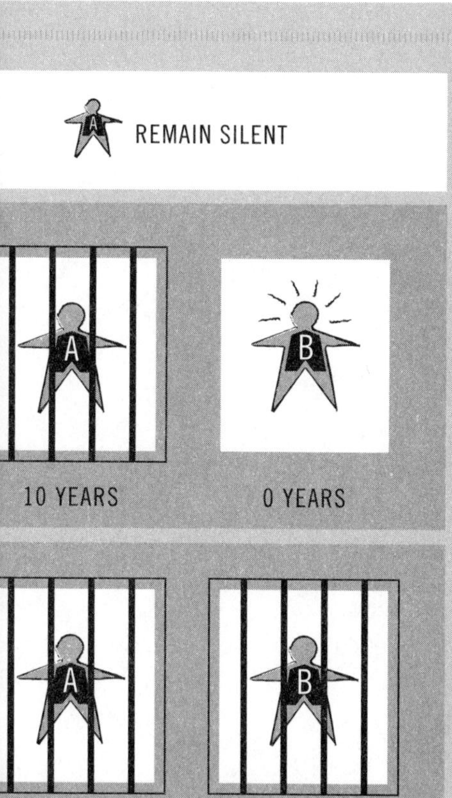
A
REMAIN SILENT
A
B
10 YEARS
0 YEARS
A
B
2 YEARS
2 YEARS

HOW TO IMPROVE OTHERS

THE DREXLER–SIBBET TEAM PERFORMANCE MODEL

HOW TO TURN A GROUP INTO A TEAM

There are hundreds of team performance models and strategies have been out there. One of the best – and also one of the simplest – was developed by Allan Drexler, founder of the consulting practice Drexler & Associates, and David Sibbet, founder of The Grove Consultants International. The model illustrates seven stages of development that a team typically goes through.

Follow the arrows in the model over the page. At every stage there is a question that we ask ourselves at that point: at the beginning of the project, 'Why am I here?'; in the middle, 'How will we do it?'; at the end, 'Why continue?' For each stage, the model describes three keys to resolving the critical issues, and some of the symptoms that mean the important issues are not resolved. For example, after having resolved stage 2 ("trust building") the group will typically experience these three "keys": mutual trust, forthrightness, reliability. Symptoms that show this stage is not yet resolved are: caution, mistrust, façade. Many of the stages seem obvious and trivial, but experience shows that every group goes through every stage. If you skip a stage, you will have to return to it later.

If you are leading a team, you should present the model at the beginning of the project. After the project has started, ask the participants at regular intervals:

- How far (i.e. at which stage of the project) are you?
- What do you need to do to reach the next stage?

If you are unsure about which stage your team is currently going through, look at the adjectives associated with each stage in the model and ask yourself which adjectives apply to you personally, and which ones apply to the team.

Don't be afraid of stirring up negative feelings among the group. An open conflict is better than one that simmers unresolved through several stages and forces you to address issues during later stages that should have been dealt with earlier.

Beware! Don't try to align your team rigidly to the model. The model is simply an aid to orientation: it is a compass, not a pacemaker.

Groups move forward only when one of the participants dares to take the first step. As leader, you should be prepared to be the first to make mistakes.

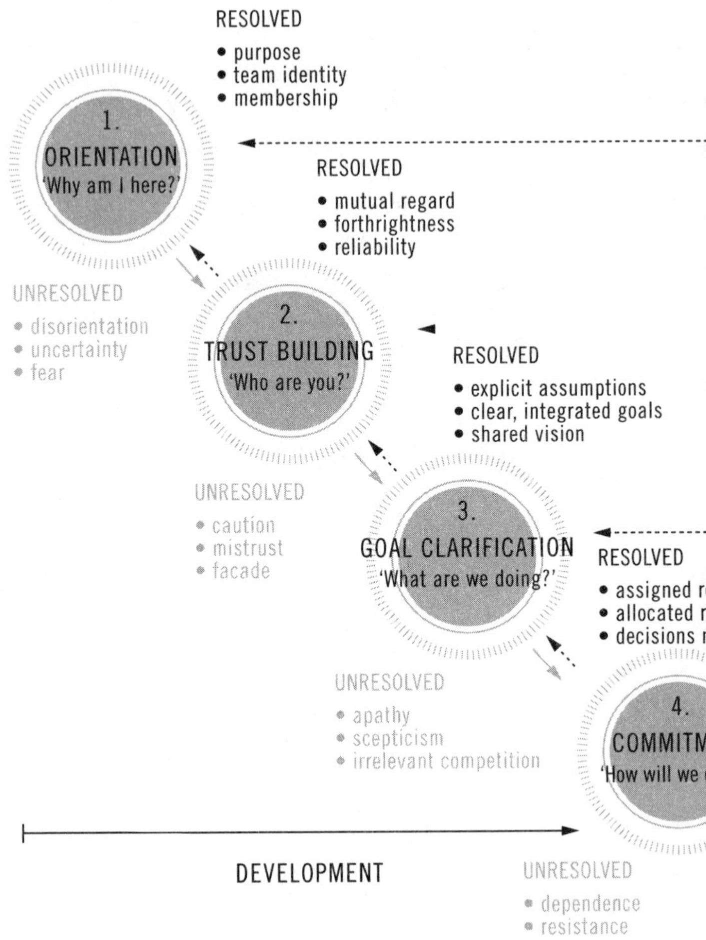

The team performance model shows the seven stages that every group goes through when carrying out a project.

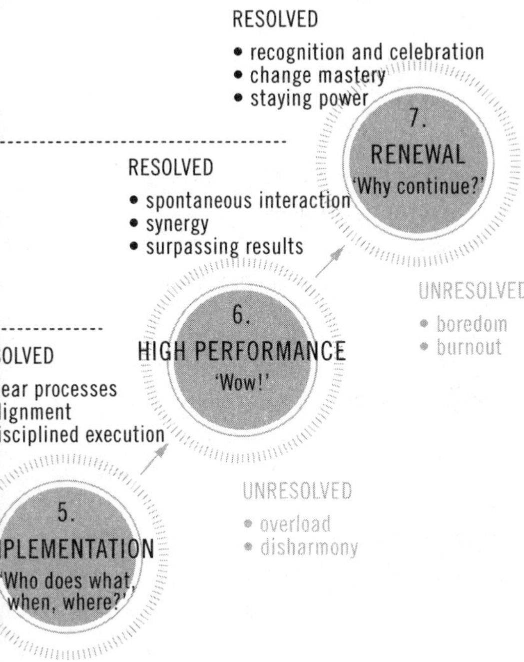
RESOLVED
• recognition and celebration
• change mastery
• staying power
7.
RENEWAL
'Why continue?'
RESOLVED
• spontaneous interaction
• synergy
• surpassing results
UNRESOLVED
• boredom
• burnout
6.
HIGH PERFORMANCE
'Wow!'
SOLVED
lear processes
lignment
isciplined execution
UNRESOLVED
• overload
• disharmony
5.
PLEMENTATION
'Who does what,
when, where?'
UNRESOLVED
• conflict/confusion
• non-alignment
• missed deadlines
PERFORMANCE

THE TEAM MODEL

IS YOUR TEAM UP TO THE JOB?

Regardless of whether you are the head of a nursery or of a national sports team, or whether you want to set up a company or a fund-raising committee, you will be asking yourself the same questions: Do I have the right people for this project? Do our skills correspond to our goals? Are we capable of doing what we want to do?

This team model will help you to judge your team. Begin by defining the skills, expertise and resources that you think are important for carrying out the project. Note the skills that are absolutely necessary for the job. Distinguish between soft skills (e.g. loyalty, motivation, reliability) and hard skills (e.g. computer, business and foreign-language abilities). For each skill, define where your critical boundary lies on a scale of zero to ten. For example, an acceptable level of fluency in French might be five. Now judge your 'players' according to these criteria. Connect the points with a line. What are the team's weaknesses, and what are their strengths?

Even more revealing than the model itself is the subsequent self-evaluation by the team members. A good team is one that can correctly judge its own capabilities.

Beware! Real strength lies in differences, not in similarities.

The best executive is the one who has sense enough to pick good men to do what he wants done, and self-restraint enough to keep from meddling with them while they do it. *Theodore Roosevelt*

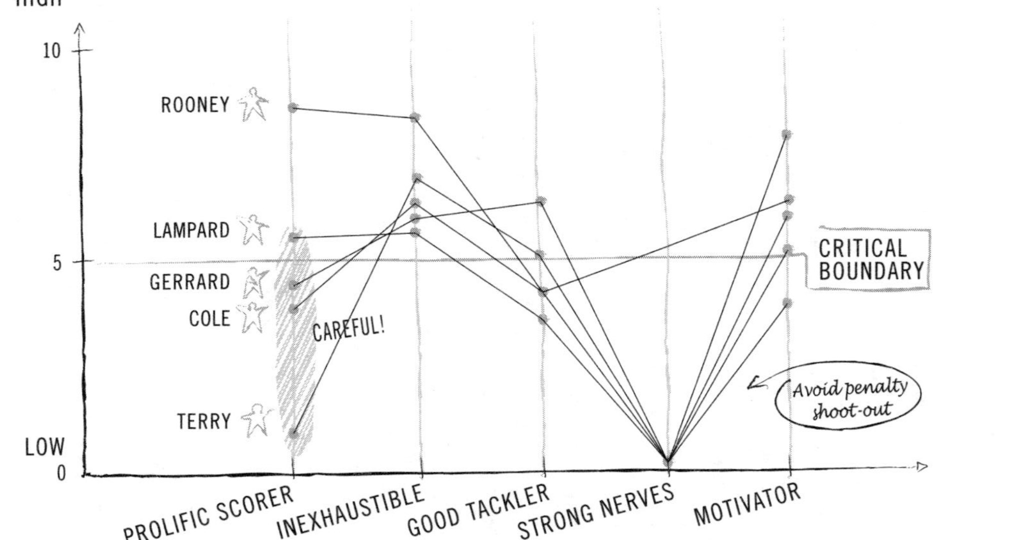

(Based on England's 2010 World Cup performance.) Create new criteria that apply to your team's objective and evaluate each team member against them. Afterwards, ask the team members to evaluate themselves. How do the curves compare?

THE GAP-IN-THE-MARKET MODEL

HOW TO RECOGNISE A BANKABLE IDEA

The goal of every new business is to discover and occupy a gap in the market. But what is the best way of proceeding? The gap-in-the-market model helps by depicting a market in a clear, three-dimensional way. Draw three axes that measure the development of your market, your customers and your future products.

Say that you want to launch a new magazine. Then:

- The x-axis is **Cost-effectiveness** – how economical is your product?
- The y-axis is **Prestige** – how well-known is the product?
- The z-axis is **Awareness** – how 'loud' is your product?

Position your competitors' products on the graph. In areas that are dense with competitors, you should enter the market with your business model only if it has the potential to be a 'category killer'. For example, *Grazia* was able to conquer the already crowded women's weekly market by combining sophisticated fashion news with strictly A-list gossip. Look for a niche, an area that has been overlooked and that is not yet occupied.

Beware! If an area is completely empty, you should check whether there is a demand there at all.

Positioning is like drilling for oil. Close is not good enough.

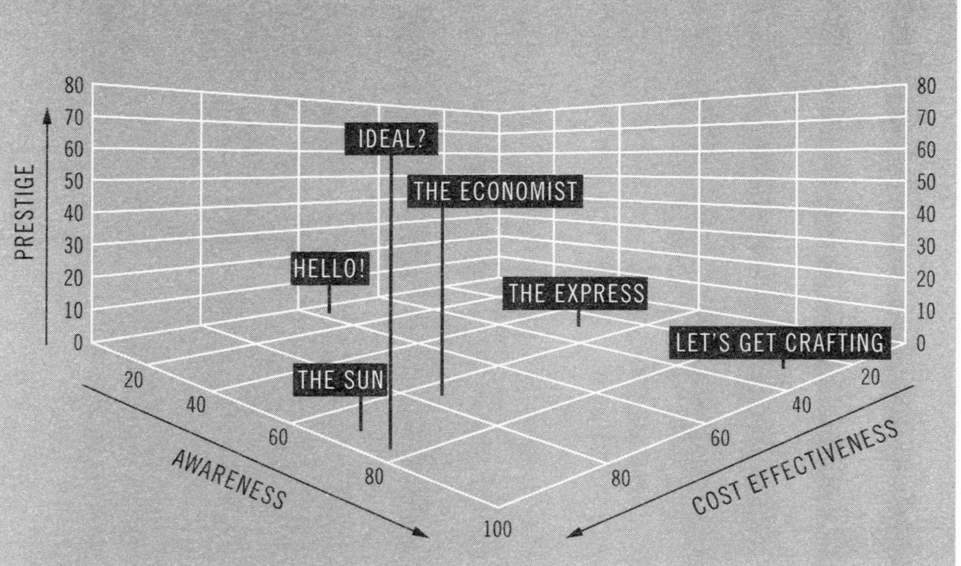

This model helps you to identify gaps in the market: position your competitors according to the three axes (e.g. prestige, cost-effectiveness, awareness). Where is there a niche?

THE HERSEY–BLANCHARD MODEL (SITUATIONAL LEADERSHIP)

HOW TO SUCCESSFULLY MANAGE YOUR EMPLOYEES

Over the last hundred years, organisational theory has taken many different turns. Man is a machine and should be treated as such (Taylor, Ford). Paying attention to social factors, and not objectively regulated working conditions, leads to the best results (Hawthorne). Organisations can regulate themselves (Clark, Farley). And strategic management, i.e. the division of organisations into primary and secondary activities, leads to success (Porter).

A rather different theory was put forward by Paul Hersey and Ken Blanchard, who suggested that the most important thing is to adapt one's style of leadership to the situation at hand. This 'situational leadership model' distinguishes between:

1. **Instructing**. When they are starting a job, employees need strong leadership. When they are new their level of commitment is usually high, but their level of expertise is still low. Employees are given orders and instructions.

2. **Coaching**. The employees' level of expertise has risen. Because of stress and the loss of the initial euphoria at starting a new job, their motivation and commitment levels have fallen. The employees are asked questions, and they look for the answers themselves.

3. **Supporting**. The level of expertise has risen sharply. The level of motivation can vary: either it has gone down (employees may resign) or it has gone up as a result of being given more independence (employees are encouraged to come up with their own ideas).

4. **Delegating**. Employees are fully in control of their work. The level of motivation is high. They are given their own projects and lead their own teams.

Lead your employees in such a way that you yourself become superfluous. And lead your employees to be successful, so that one day they will be in a leadership position themselves.

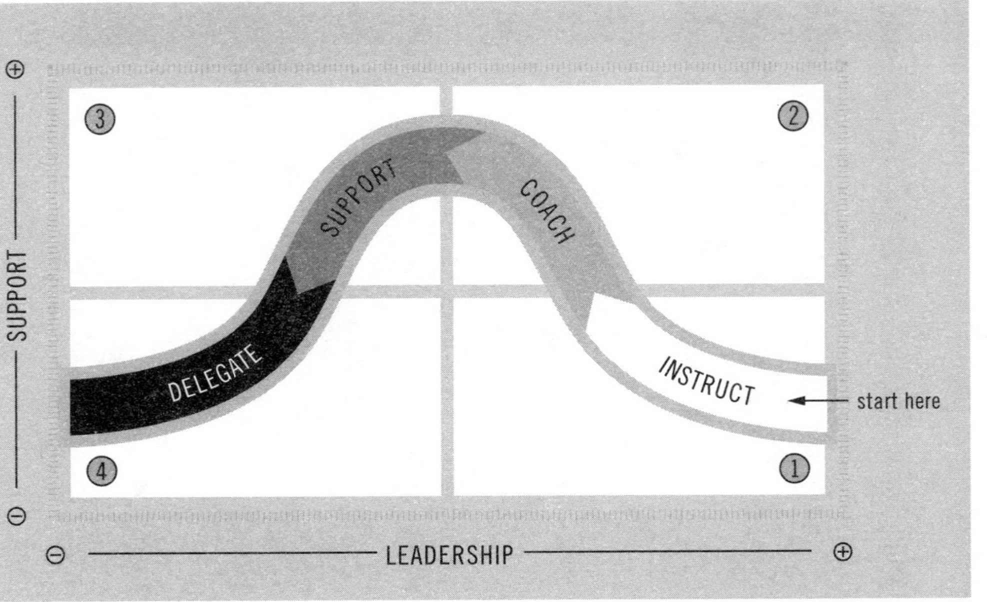

Read from right to left. New employees must first be instructed, then coached, then supported, and finally delegated to.

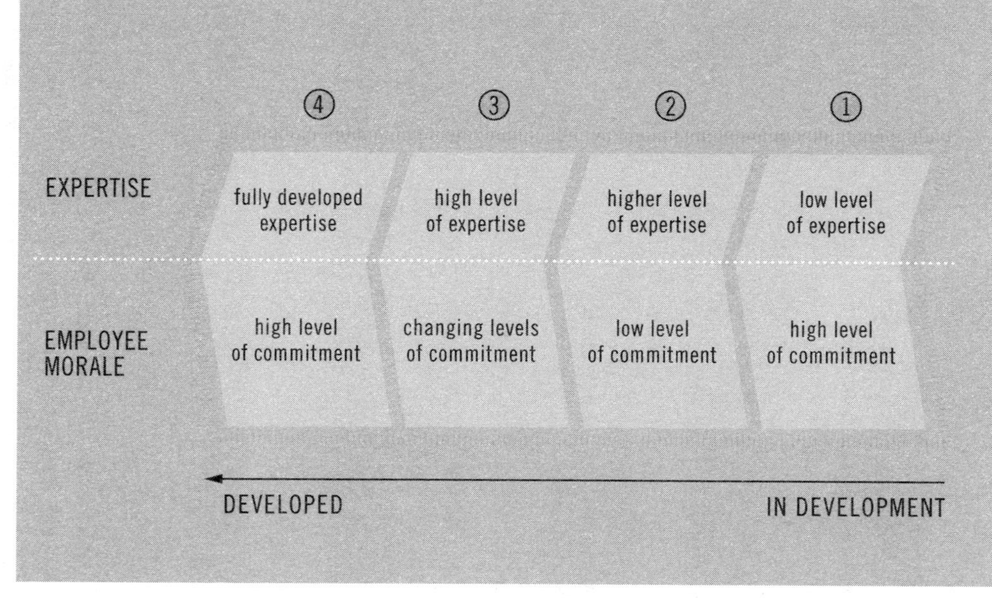

Read from right to left. The ratio of competence to work ethic on a time axis.

THE ROLE-PLAYING MODEL (BELBIN & DE BONO)

HOW TO CHANGE YOUR OWN POINT OF VIEW

When the creative thinking guru Edward de Bono presented his 'six thinking hats' in 1986, critics dismissed the idea as just a bit of fun. De Bono's idea was to assign the members of a working group a temporary one-dimensional point of view or 'thinking hat'. Today, the technique is widely accepted, and De Bono's six hats are used as a team or meeting technique to stimulate communication and create a playful/serious approach to a discussion topic.

This is how it works. An idea or a strategy is discussed by the members of a group. During the discussion, all the members adopt one of the six points of view – reflected in the colour of the hat. (It is important that all members of the group wear the same colour hat at the same time.)

These are the characteristics associated with each colour:

- **White hat**: analytical, objective thinking, the emphasis is on facts and feasibility.
- **Red hat**: emotional thinking, subjective feelings, perceptions and opinions.
- **Black hat**: critical thinking, risk assessment, identifying problems, scepticism, critique.
- **Yellow hat**: optimistic thinking, speculative best-case scenario.
- **Green hat**: creative, associative thinking, new ideas, brainstorming, constructive.
- **Blue hat**: structured thinking, process overview, the big picture.

Beware! The meeting must be moderated to ensure that the team members do not slip out of their designated role.

Homogenous teams, i.e. teams in which the members have similar views and character traits, don't work as well. In the 1970s, Meredith Belbin studied individuals and character roles and their influence on group processes. Based on his observations, he identified nine different profiles:

- **Action-oriented**: do-er, implementer, perfectionist.
- **Communication-oriented**: co-ordinator, team player, trailblazer.
- **Knowledge-oriented**: innovator, observer, specialist.

If you have a good idea, but fear that it may meet with strong resistance, try to lead the discussion in such a way that the other members of the group think that they came up with the idea themselves. The more people feel they have originated an idea, the more passionately they fight for its implementation. If nobody claims to have come up with the idea, perhaps it wasn't that good in the first place!

I never did anything alone. What was accomplished, was accomplished collectively. *Golda Meir*

→See also: Drexler–Sibbet team performance model (p.130)

TEAM ROLE	CONTRIBUTION
The plant	introduces new ideas
Resource investigator	investigates possibilities develops contacts
Co-ordinator	encourages decision-mak processes, delegates
Shaper	overcomes obstacles
Monitor	examines feasibility
Team worker	improves communication gets things moving
Implementor	puts ideas into practice
Completer	ensures optimal results
Specialist	provides specialist know

ARACTER	PERMISSIBLE WEAKNESS
rthodox thinking	absent-minded
munificative, extrovert	over-optimistic
ependent, responsible	appears manipulative
amic, works well er pressure	impatient, provocative
l-headed, strategic, critical	uninspired
perative, diplomatic	indecisive
iplined, reliable, effective	inflexible
scientious, prompt	timid, hardly delegates
-reliant, committed	gets lost in the details

THE RESULT OPTIMISATION MODEL

WHY THE PRINTER ALWAYS BREAKS DOWN JUST BEFORE A DEADLINE

There are many project management models and methods. Most of them are based on the premise that there is a fixed amount of time in which to carry out a project. Generally, within this time, ideas are gathered (G) and consolidated (C), and a concept is selected and implemented (I). In real life we all know that we never have enough time. And the little time we do have is reduced by unforeseen events like a printer breaking down the minute you want to use it.

The result optimisation model divides the available time into three sequences (loops) of equal length, thereby forcing the project manager to complete the project three times. The idea is to improve the outcome in each successive working loop. This method leads not only to improved output quality but also to a more successful final outcome: at the end of a project, instead of simply being glad that it is 'finally put to bed', the whole team has a threefold feeling of achievement.

Beware! Be stringent when carrying out this strategy: work in such a way that each loop is properly completed before embarking on the next. Otherwise this model loses its dynamic.

With development processes, it is important to clearly separate the three stages, of gathering, consolidation and implementation.

A beautiful thing is never perfect. *Anonymous*

➥See also: Drexler–Sibbet team performance model (p.130)

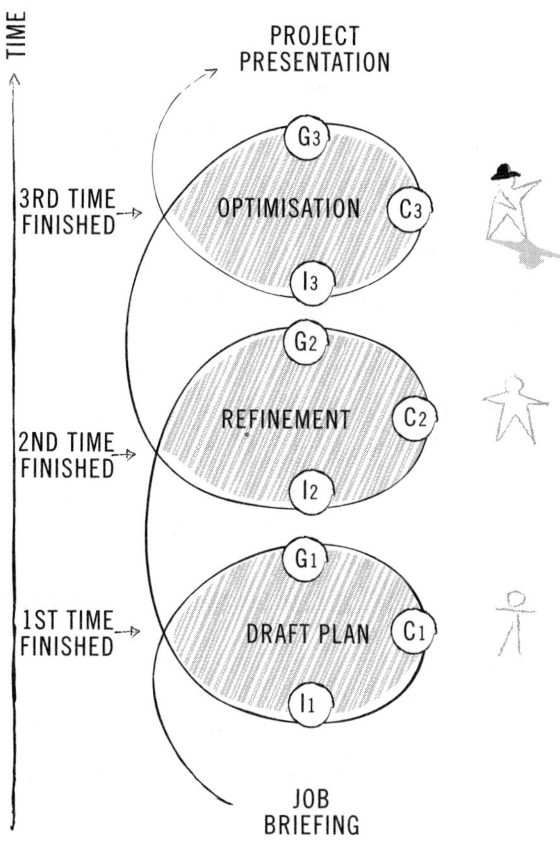

G = GATHER IDEAS
V = CONSOLIDATE INTO A CONCEPT
I = IMPLEMENT

To achieve an optimal result, you should plan your project so that it is 'finished' three times. After the third time it really is finished.

THE WORLD'S NEXT TOP MODEL

WHAT CAN WE LEARN FROM THIS BOOK?

Even when it comes to making the simplest decision, the number of factors to be taken into account can exceed our powers of imagination. Therefore management models have tried to reduce complexity by condensing ideas into a matrix with four fields.

'It all started with spreadsheet programmes,' explains Karin Frick, head of research at the Gottlieb Duttweiler institute. Spreadsheets are among the most powerful management tools of recent years. Spreadsheet software such as Microsoft's Excel have revolutionised the way in which we manage expenses and budgets.

'To a man with a hammer, everything looks like a nail.' This observation of Mark Twain's can also be applied to models, which tend to create their own reality. Four-field matrices and Excel spreadsheets give their users a way of viewing, understanding and organising the world. They have changed the way we understand business processes as drastically as the telescope changed the way we look at the sky. When they were introduced, spreadsheets and matrices were new visual aids which offered companies a way of viewing reality from a new perspective. But the reality was more complex than the models would lead us to believe.

The next top model was introduced in the 1970s by Frederic Vester. He popularised the idea of networked thinking. Since then there has been a succession of best-sellers on the topic of 'managing complex systems', e.g. Kevin Kelly's *Out of Control* in the 1990s, and *The Black Swan* by Nassim Nicholas Taleb in 2007. How to handle complex situations, systematic thinking, chaos theory and self-organisation theory have been compulsory reading for managers for years.

Yet management theory today is at about the same stage as medicine was before the introduction of X-ray technology and, more recently, computer tomography. Before then, doctors were largely unable to penetrate beyond symptoms to the underlying causes, and their treatment methods were correspondingly primitive and imprecise. The development of the new techniques made possible increasingly precise procedures. And soon, genetic engineering may enable us to tackle the causes of diseases directly.

The type of analysis now used in genetic engineering is promising new insights in the area of management. The programs that are being developed for the decryption of genetic information and for the early detection of diseases will, in future, also help to decipher patterns in buying behaviour and other information flows. In *Super Crunchers*, Ian Ayres shows how this is already possible today. Here are some examples he gives:

- On the basis of statistical analyses of the weather data in the Bordeaux wine-growing region, the economist Orley Ashenfelter can predict the quality of new vintages more accurately than the wine guru Robert Parker, who relies on his intuition, tastebuds and experience.
- Online customers of the credit card company Capital One receive a computer-generated answer before they even have a chance to ask a question, based on an analysis of questions and answers asked by users of the same kind of credit card they have. Only then can they choose an alternative question from the menu. (Apparently Visa is already able to predict divorces on the basis of credit-card data.)
- Harrah's Casinos can predict when a punter's 'losing pain threshold' will be reached. When the program gives a warning,

> a 'luck ambassador' is sent off to entice the loser with a gift before it is too late – in the hope that they will stay and carry on losing.

Today, the results of certain decisions are first tested in a virtual world before they are implemented in real markets – a kind of market test *in silico*. Nowadays, almost everything we do, buy and decide leaves behind electronic traces (by means of RFID tags, people and products can be relatively easily located in space and time). In this way, companies are able to monitor how their business is running, where their customers (or employees) are, what they are currently doing and even how they are feeling.

In the future, decision-makers will work with prognosis tools (as described above) rather than with models. But there is a problem: decision-makers using such tools in the present do not understand what they are calculating. The formulas and models that explain the world are black boxes, understood by only a few experts. The typical user has to trust the system without understanding it. But although we may not know exactly what the models are calculating, we can still test, measure and refine them with real customer and market data.

Does this mean that you can forget all the models you have encountered in this book? On the contrary. The value of these early models should not be underestimated: in an increasingly confusing and chaotic world, they help us to focus on what is important and to believe in what we see. Even with the newest medical inventions to hand, a doctor will still rely on the most basic diagnostic tools: listening to and examining the patient.

The models in this book give us a way of looking at the world.

➥See also: Black box model (p.118)

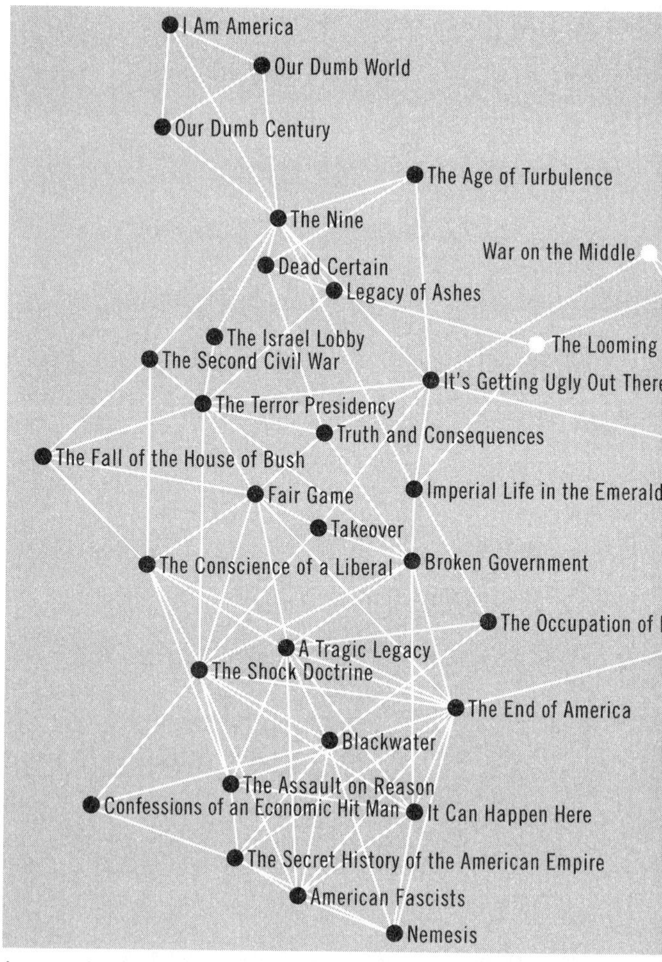

An example of a dynamic model by Valdis Krebs: it illustrates buying behaviour for political books: liberal content (black), conservative content (grey) and books with no political agenda (white). Most readers stick to one of the three groups.

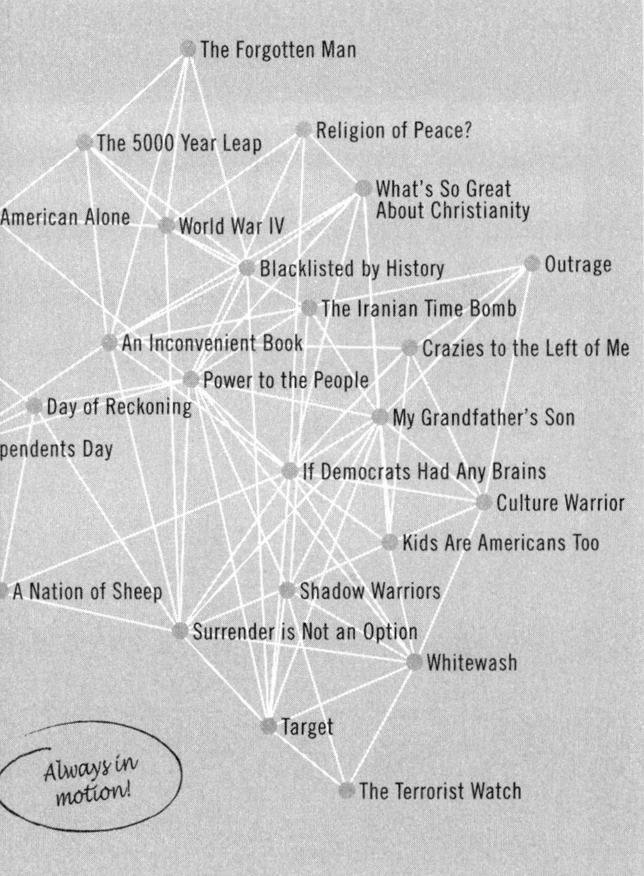
The Forgotten Man
The 5000 Year Leap
Religion of Peace?
What's So Great About Christianity
American Alone
World War IV
Blacklisted by History
Outrage
The Iranian Time Bomb
An Inconvenient Book
Crazies to the Left of Me
Power to the People
Day of Reckoning
My Grandfather's Son
ependents Day
If Democrats Had Any Brains
Culture Warrior
Kids Are Americans Too
A Nation of Sheep
Shadow Warriors
Surrender is Not an Option
Whitewash
Target
Always in motion!
The Terrorist Watch

NOW IT'S YOUR TURN

DRAWING LESSON 1

WHY YOU SHOULD DRAW WHILE YOU TALK

Models work best if you draw them. Why? Do an experiment: speak in front of an audience about a subject and look to see how many of the listeners make notes during your lecture. Give the same talk again – to a different audience – and while you are speaking draw models for them that roughly illustrate your thoughts. How many of the listeners copy the models? How many make notes this time?

These are the advantages of giving ideas a visual form:

- The audience does not just listen to you, it also looks at what you are doing – you receive twice as much attention.
- Attention is directed from your person to your subject. You are no longer standing in front of a jury, you are speaking with the jury about a separate issue.
- Images are always remembered in connection with feelings and places. Your listeners will look at the model and remember your lecture.

You can only draw stick-men? Not to worry. The more sophisticated and perfect a drawing is, the more alienating it is. With simple, clear drawings the audience gets the feeling that they could do this too. So stick with your stick-men – this doesn't require you to be a talented artist – but keep developing them.

A
?

DRAWING LESSON 2

HOW TO MAKE A BIG IMPRESSION WITH LITTLE TRICKS

- **Draw while you talk.** When they are drawn in real time, even imprecise or arbitrary elements are understood by the viewer – and treated more leniently.
- **Pictures say more than a thousand words.** Draw an iceberg to draw attention to a growing problem, a temple if you want to illustrate pillars of success, a bridge to show connections, rough outlines of countries to establish a geographical context, a conveyor belt for procedures and processes, a funnel if you want to consolidate ideas, a pyramid for a hierarchy.
- **Familiar but different.** Everyone understands traffic signs – or the play and pause button signs on the remote control. Even better: surprise your audience by turning traditional symbols (e.g. $) or abbreviations (e.g. 't' for time) into pictograms.
- **Create structure.** If you have to discuss important but unconnected ideas, write them down and circle each one. But don't create unnecessary connections between the circles, e.g. by overlapping them or linking them with arrows.
- **Wrong but strong.** If you draw a crooked line, don't go back and correct it, because the line of your argument will then be interrupted. The same applies if your circles come out looking like eggs. These are abstract illustrations, not works of art.

10%
USA
EU
AFR
A
B
C
A3
A1
A2
TNT

MY MODELS

APPENDIX

BIBLIOGRAPHY

Becker, Udo: *The Continuum Encyclopedia of Symbols.* Continuum, 2000

Bourdieu, Pierre: *Distinction: A Social Critique of the Judgement of Taste*, Harvard University Press, 1984

Esquire: *The Big Black Book*, Hearst Corporation, 2007

Gladwell, Malcolm: *The Tipping Point.* Black Day Books, 2002

Kelley, Tom: *The Art of Innovation.* Currency, 2000

Klein, Naomi: *The Shock Doctrine.* Metropolitan Books, 2007

Koch, Richard: *The 80/20 Principle. The Secret of Achieving More with Less.* Doubleday Business, 1997

MacRone, Michael and Lulevitch, Tom: *Eureka! What Archimedes Really Meant and 80 Other Key Ideas Explained.* HarperCollins, 1994

Mankiw, N. Gregory: *Macroeconomics.* Worth Publishers, 1997

Reason, James: 'Human error: models and management', *British Medical Journal*, 18 March 2000, 320:768–70

Senge, Peter: *The Fifth Discipline.* Currency, 2006

Stroebe, Wolfgang, Hewstone, Miles and Stephenson, Geoffrey M.: *Introduction to Social Psychology: A European Perspective.* Blackwell, 1996

Taleb, Nassim Nicholas: *The Black Swan: The Impact of the Highly Improbable*. Random House, 2007

Whitmore, John: *Coaching for Performance*, 4th revised edition. Nicholas Brealey Publishing, 2009

Wired, Condé Nast, 2008

ON THE INTERNET

Swiss cheese model: www.pubmedcentral.nih.gov/articlerender.fcgi?artid=1117770

BCG matrix: www.12manage.com/methods_bcgmatrix.html

Morphological box: www.zwicky-stiftung.ch

Do-it-yourself business graphics: www.billiondollargraphics.com

A periodic table of visualisation methods: www.visual-literacy.org/periodic_table/periodic_table.html

Management models: www.provenmodels.com

Predictive models: islandia.law.yale.edu/ayres/predictionTools.htm

APPENDIX

ILLUSTRATION CREDITS

The following sources were utilised for the creation of illustrations for this book.

Swiss cheese model: James Reason, www.pubmedcentral.nih.gov/articlerender.fcgi?artid=1117770

Gap-in-the-market model: www.innovation-aktuell.de

The chasm: Malcolm Gladwell, *The Tipping Point.* Black Day Books, 2002

Gift model: Esquire, *The Big Black Book.* Hearst Communications, 2007

Uffe Elbæk model: Uffe Elbæk, *Kaospilot A-Z.* KaosCommunication, 2003

The SuperMemo-Model, *Wired*, Condé Nast, 2008

Fashion model: Eric Sommier, *Mode, le monde en movement.* Village Mondial, 2000

Fashion model 2: *Esquire, The Big Black Book.* Hearst Communications, 2007

Flow model: Mihaly Csikszentmihalyi: *Creativity: Flow and the Psychology of Discovery and Invention.* Harper Perennial, 1996

Sinus Milieu: www.sinus-sociovision.de

Bourdieu model: Pierre Bourdieu, *Die feinen Unterschiede: Kritik der gesellschaftlichen Urteilskraft.* Suhrkamp, 2000

Prisoner's dilemma: Làszlò Mérő, *Die Logik der Vernunft, Spieltheorie und die Psychologie des Handelns.* Rowohlt, 2000

Thinking outside the box: www.interchange.dk, Toke Mœller, Monica Nissen

Maslow pyramid: Gottlieb Duttweiler Institut

The Hype Cycle: Gartner, 2010

Political compass: www.politicalcompass.org

Hersey and Blanchard: Paul Hersey, Kenneth H. Blanchard & Dewey E. Johnson, *Management of Organizational Behavior: Leading Human Resources.* Pearson Education, 2008

Drexler–Sibbet: www.grove.com

Team role model: www.belbin.com

Consequences model: Søren Christensen and Kristian Kreiner, *Projektledelse i 1œst koblede systemer.* Jurist- og Økonomforbundets Forlag, 2002

Whitmore model: John Withmore, *Coaching für die Praxis.* Heyne, 1997

Cognitive dissonance: Carlo Tavris and Elliot Aronson: *Mistakes Were Made (But Not by Me).* Harcourt, 2007

The world's next top model: www.orgnet.com/divided.html

APPENDIX

FINAL NOTE

This is the first book to set out a wide range of decision-making strategies and models. We had no prototypes, so we had to break new ground. If you come across mistakes, if you know of other, better models, if you have suggestions of how a model can be further developed, or if you simply want to make a comment, please write to us. You can discuss the models at www.2topmodels.com.

THANKS

The writing of this book would not have been possible without the generous help of the following people and institutions:

Pat Ammon, Multiple Global Design (for the Morphological box); Chris Anderson, *Wired* (for the SuperMemo, the Long tail and the Superficial knowledge models); Mark Buchanan (for the Subtle signals model); Andreas 'Becks' Dietrich (for intelligent sparring); Uffe Elbæk (for his ability to draw anything, as well as for the Uffe Elbæk model); Matt Fischer, Apple Music Store (for inspiration); Karin Frick, GDI (for a glimpse into the future); Dag Grœdal, Nordea (for helpful suggestions); Peter Haag (because he believed [in] us); Cedric Hiltbrand (for his corrections); the Kaospilot University (for the best education imaginable); Marc Kaufmann (for positive disrespectfulness); Benno Maggi (for the Family tree, Gap-in-the-market and Swiss cheese models, as well as for continuous feedback); Christian Nill (for feedback); Courtney Page-Ferell, Play (for the advice 'Don't take yourself too seriously'); Sven Opitz, University of Basel (for Double-loop learning); Lisa Owens and Daniel Crewe, Profile Books (for great editing and making all of this possible), Jenny Piening (for careful and smart translation), Mark Raskino, Gartner (for the hype cycle), Sara Schindler and Laura Clemens (for editing and proofreading); Pierre-André Schmid (for his ongoing interest and the many books); Michael Schuler, Head of Music, DRS3 (for helping with the Music matrix); Ute Tellmann, University of Basel (for criticism of the models); and Daniel Weber, *NZZ Folio* (for helpful advice).

APPENDIX

THE AUTHORS

Mikael Krogerus, born in 1976 in Stockholm, is a Finnish citizen and grew up in Sweden and Germany. He studied politics at the Freie Universität in Berlin and completed his studies in 2003 at the Kaospilot School in Denmark. He went on to work for the youth TV show *Chat the Planet* in New York, and from 2005 was an editor at *NZZ Folio*, the magazine of the *Neue Züricher Zeitung*. Since 2009 he has been working as a freelance journalist for *Der Freitag*, *Brand Eins* and the *NZZ*, among others.

Roman Tschäppeler, born in 1978 in Bern, worked for the Swiss idea factory BrainStore and founded a cultural centre as a teenager. In 2003 he completed his studies at the Kaospilot School in Denmark and developed numerous cookbooks for a top Swiss chef, for whom he also acts as manager. In 2004 he founded the communication agency 'guzo', which develops campaigns for companies and aid organisations, produces music, and provides consulting services in the area of idea and innovation implementation.

Philip Earnhart is a freelance art director. He was born in 1965 in Switzerland, is an American citizen and grew up in Switzerland and the USA. In 1989 he completed his studies at the Art Institute of Seattle. He went on to work for advertising agencies in the USA and Europe and developed infographics and learning aids for Citigroup, Delta Airlines, DuPont and KPMG, among others. Since 2006 he has been living with his family in Switzerland.

Jenny Piening is a freelance translator, editor and writer based in Berlin.

The original edition was published in 2008 under the title
50 Erfolgsmodelle, kleines Handbuch für strategische Entscheidungen by
Kein & Aber, Zürich.

First American Edition 2012

Printed in the United States of America

For information about permission to reproduce selections from this book, write
to Permissions, W. W. Norton & Company, Inc.,
500 Fifth Avenue, New York, NY 10110

For information about special discounts for bulk purchases, please contact
W. W. Norton Special Sales at specialsales@wwnorton.com
or 800-233-4830

Manufacturing by Courier Westford

Library of Congress Cataloging-in-Publication Data

Krogerus, Mikael.
[50 Erfolgsmodelle. English]
The decision book : fifty models for strategic thinking / Mikael Krogerus, Roman
Tschäppeler ; translated by Jenny Piening ; with illustrations by Philip Earnhart.
– 1st American ed.
p. cm.
"The original edition was published in 2008 under the title 50 Erfolgsmodelle,
kleines Handbuch für strategische Entscheidungen by Kein & Aber, Zürich."
Includes bibliographical references.
ISBN 978-0-393-07961-6 (hbk.)
1. Decision making. 2. Critical thinking. I. Tschäppeler, Roman.
II. Piening, Jenny. III. Title.
BF448.K7613 2012
153.8'3–dc23

2011041446

W. W. Norton & Company, Inc.
500 Fifth Avenue, New York, N.Y. 10110
www.wwnorton.com

W. W. Norton & Company Ltd.
Castle House, 75/76 Wells Street, London W1T 3QT

4 5 6 7 8 9 0